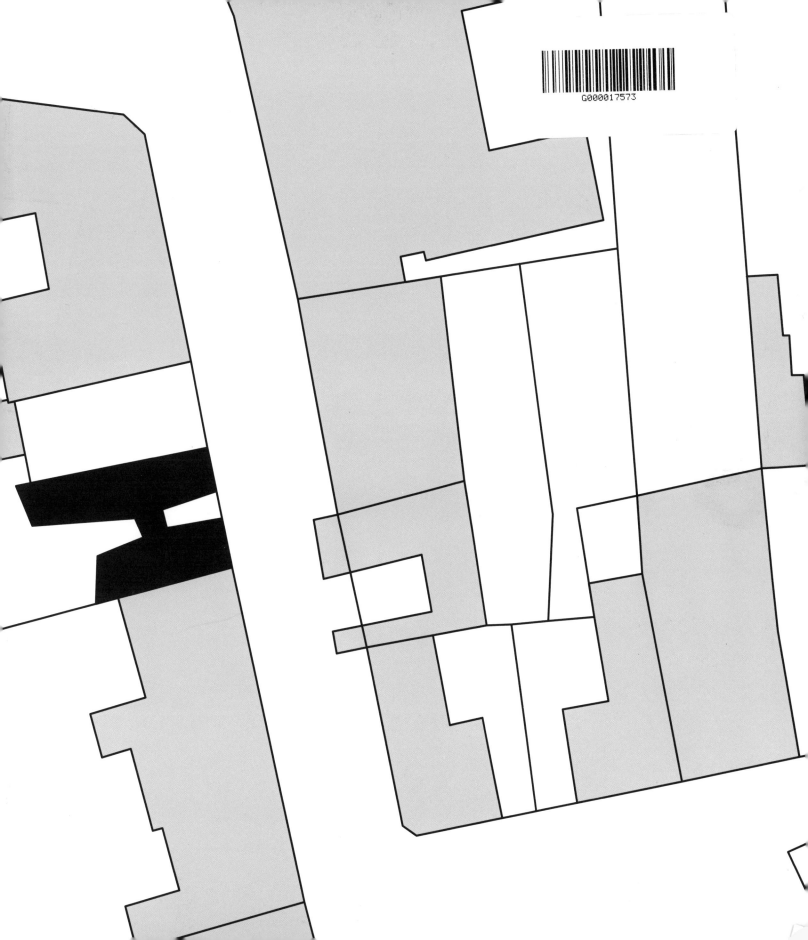

INFILL
New Houses for Urban Sites

LAURENCE KING

Published in 2009
by Laurence King Publishing Ltd
361–373 City Road
London EC1V 1LR
Tel +44 (0)20 7841 6900
Fax +44 (0)20 7841 6910
e-mail enquiries@laurenceking.co.uk
www.laurenceking.co.uk

A catalogue record for this book is available from the British Library.

ISBN-13: 978-1-85669-558-9

Designed by www.hoopdesign.co.uk

Printed in China

Site plans were specially drawn based on information supplied by the architects.
All site plans are oriented north.

INFILL
New Houses for Urban Sites

Adam Mornement
&
Annabel Biles

LAURENCE KING PUBLISHING

CONTENTS

4
UNDERGROUND & PARTIALLY SUBMERGED SITES

5
SLOPING SITES

INTRODUCTION

One of the working titles for this book was *Curious Footprints*, in recognition of the increasingly weird and wonderful shapes of contemporary urban homes. In recent years, houses on thin slivers of abandoned land, on precipitous hillsides and even in alleyways, have proliferated in the pages of architecture and lifestyle magazines around the world. To a certain breed of developer and city dweller, bringing life to awkwardly shaped sites in unprepossessing locations has almost become a badge of honour. The title was abandoned, but the phenomenon shows no signs of abating, as the 40 examples of new urban houses in this book demonstrate.

The selected title, *Infill*, is an industry term for the development of small-scale vacant parcels of land within built-up areas. In space-constricted Western cities the level of construction on infill sites is unprecedented. Anything is up for grabs. Every postage stamp-sized parcel of land is in demand. Of the examples in this book, the Love House in Yokohama, Japan (page 138) is the house with the smallest footprint (24 square metres / 258 square feet).

The forces behind this phenomenon are many and varied. To some degree it can be read as a response to government policies in the United States, western Europe, Japan and elsewhere on the reuse of urban land in preference to building on previously undeveloped land on urban fringes. Other factors include international obligations to reduce carbon emissions which have impacted on the materials and technologies used to build new houses, as well as on location and lifestyle preferences; shrinking household sizes and ageing populations mean there is greater demand for single-unit accommodation in and around city centres. Another pressure is that growing numbers of us are gravitating towards city centres, lured by work opportunities and access to amenities and entertainment. Between 1990 and 2000, for instance, the population of New York grew by 9.4 per cent, equating to 685,714 people,[1] and given the city's geographic limitations, it is not difficult to

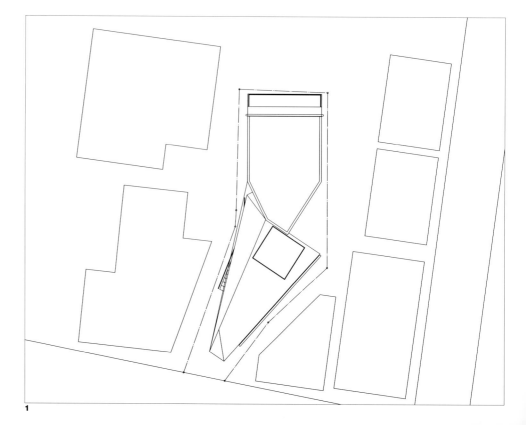

2

1 Curious footprint: intense demand for urban land is resulting in houses with increasingly unusual footprints, such as the Wedge House (2005) in Tokyo, by Milligram Architectural Studio.

2 This house (1 metre/3 feet wide at its narrowest point) occupies a narrow alley in Madre de Deus, Brazil. Since its construction the house has become a local tourist attraction.

3 The Anderson House (2002) in central London, by Jamie Fobert Architects, has no external elevations. It occupies a 7 metre (23 foot) deep shaft enclosed by offices and mansion blocks.

imagine the heightened level of interest in the city's infill sites that this population influx provoked.

Of course, finding ways to develop small parcels of urban land is nothing new. It is part of the physiological evolution of cities, and always has been. The reason for writing a book about it today is because the phenomenon has intensified, and the architectural outcomes are increasingly fascinating.

Finding an infill

Every urban area, however small or loosely defined, is constantly exposed to a diverse cocktail of pressures. Depending on time and place, these may include economic fluctuations, demographic change, terrorist activity, revised building codes, new construction technologies and shifts in rates of taxation. All of these factors, and many others besides, have the potential either to create new infill sites or the conditions for the cultivation of existing spaces. The convergence of two of these factors led to the creation of the world's first multi-storey reinforced-concrete buildings.

Towards the end of the nineteenth century, authorities governing industrialized cities,

3

including Paris and London, were exploring ways to maximize land values. In Paris this found expression in a 1902 building code that allowed, among other things, increased height limits. At around the same time, architects were beginning to experiment with reinforced concrete as a construction material. In 1903 Belgian-born architect Auguste Perret, whose work later became an inspiration to Le Corbusier, designed an apartment building for a tall, narrow site at 25b Rue Franklin in Paris, harnessing the new technologies and exploiting the recent code. It was the building that established Perret's reputation, and it would have been impossible to build only ten years earlier.

Among the most common reasons for small parcels of land in built-up areas becoming available for development are the collapse of existing buildings, and obsolescence. Once a building has outlived its practical life, there is an opportunity to replace it. That sounds simple enough, but in built-up areas characterized by buildings of a certain architectural style or use, the process of designing and constructing a replacement is not always straightforward.

A single-storey house in Melbourne, Australia had stood vacant for almost 40 years. The owner had been paying his rates, so the authorities had no reason to track him down, but as the years passed the structural integrity of the house declined. Eventually, after concerted attempts to alert the owner, the local council demolished the house, leaving only the front façade propped up by steel posts. A few years later the land was sold and the new owners began the process of securing consent for the removal of the façade, to clear space for a new architect-designed infill. A tug of war ensued: the planning authorities claimed that the Victorian integrity of the street would be compromised, while the owners regarded the retention of the façade as a nonsensical barrier to optimizing the dimensions of the small site. Two years later the owners won permission to

4

5

6

proceed. The result is a discreet and delicately proportioned house popular with the local community and well suited to twenty-first-century family life (see 302 Station Street, page 20).

Architect Manuel de las Casas was similarly hamstrung by building codes, though perhaps for more understandable reasons, when designing a new house in the historic Spanish city of Toledo (see Sánchez Medina House, page 28), while Monty Ravenscroft had reluctant neighbours, tree preservation specialists, sceptical mortgage lenders and the local council to contend with when trying to get his house built on a narrow dog-leg of land between two Georgian villas in a south London conservation area (see 15½ Consort Road, page 172).

In neighbourhoods without such a defined sense of identity, the process can be easier and the design shackles looser. Albuixech is a small farming community about 15 kilometres (nine miles) from Valencia. It is a place with few airs or graces. Property is affordable and the commute to the bright city lights is easy. It is the sort of place young couples move to when they want

to get on the housing ladder, or start a family. One such couple bought a partially derelict early-twentieth-century mid-terrace property, had it demolished and asked up-and-coming architect Manuel Cerdá Pérez to design a new house for them. With few planning constraints to stunt his creative ambition, he designed a house with a façade of woven metal (see AAG House, page 24). The outcome has become a local landmark.

In some cases a certain amount of lateral thinking is required to identify an infill. A family in the French town of Vichy wanted to build a new house close to the town centre, but found that residential buildings in a suitable state of disrepair were few and far between. So they decided to look at derelict industrial buildings and apply for a rezoning permit (see Family House in Vichy, page 32). There are also occasions where the ground floor of a site is not vacant at all. For instance, in Lyons, 120 kilometres (75 miles) southeast of Vichy, a new five-storey family house has been built on top of a two-storey restaurant, filling in a volume left over from the area's nineteenth-century industrial past (see Duong House, page 74).

4 25b rue Franklin (1903), Paris. Auguste Perret took advantage of changes to building codes and advances in construction technology to design one of the world's first multi-storey reinforced-concrete buildings.

5 House on rue Robert Blanche (1997), Paris. By the end of the twentieth century the construction of multi-storey infills on narrow plots was no longer unusual. This four-storey infill, designed by Architecture Studio, was built on top of an existing ground floor.

6 The Maison Saint-Cyr (1900) in Brussels, a five-storey infill that occupies a 4 metre (13 foot) wide plot, is an Art Nouveau landmark. It was designed by Gustave Strauven.

7 45 rue Louis Blanc (2006), Paris. Municipal governments are often the only bodies with the financial muscle to develop large-scale, long-term redundant sites. The site in the centre of the image, in the tenth arrondissement, was developed for social housing by architects Emmanuel Combarel and Dominique Marrec.

7

The ability to identify improbable sites can have significant financial benefits. When building a residential infill it is generally an accepted rule of thumb that approximately 50 per cent of the cost will go on the land, with the remainder going on the building. But if the land is not considered to be particularly desirable, that ratio can shift dramatically, as it did for the Japanese couple who commissioned architect Shuhei Endo to design a house on a rocky hill face sandwiched between a road and a railway (see Rooftecture S, page 208). For them, the land cost of the site was closer to 20 per cent of the total.

The economics of infill

The process of building a house on an infill site is comparable to any residential development. Depending on local conditions, it will involve an assessment of how and under what terms the land can be acquired; information should be gathered on the history and physical character of the land, such as topography, subsoil, drainage, access, the presence of any environmental contaminants and heritage regulations. And, of course, the cost implications of all these issues must be considered. It is because of this last point that many infill sites stand empty for so many years.

The economics of infill sites are notoriously complex. We are not talking about expansive, edge-of-town greenfield sites primed for development by big-budget house builders who can make large profits by rolling out the same design models on multiple units with minimal site preparation costs; infill sites often require expensive and time-consuming remediation works. As already discussed, they are also likely to be constrained by planning requirements, which may limit their height, bulk and marketability – gardens and outdoor areas are rare luxuries in urban infills. In short, it can be very difficult to develop a viable financial package to revive an infill site. The returns are often too slim to appeal to developers, and the costs often prohibitively high for individuals.

In high-cost urban areas, one-off private homes built on long-term redundant sites are a relatively exclusive breed. It is more common to find multi-unit infill schemes, perhaps developed by or with the support of a government or municipal authority. It is even more common to find multi-use infill schemes that are often part of larger regeneration programmes for a run-down area.

Diversifying returns from commercial and office uses, as well as residential rents and sales, can be a way of involving the private sector in public schemes. A recent example of such an approach with a particularly spectacular architectural outcome is the Spittelau Viaduct development in Vienna, designed by Zaha Hadid Architects. This serpentine complex of apartments, offices and artists' studios, elevated on stilts above a busy road and canal, weaves in and out of the arches of a heritage-protected viaduct designed by Otto Wagner.

Governments, municipal authorities and development corporations are often the only organizations with the financial muscle to tackle the revival of large and intractable infill sites, but for smaller parcels there are other approaches, such as developing a replicable model for houses on one-off plots, as attempted by architects Brian Johnsen and Sebastien Schmaling in Milwaukee. The idea makes perfect sense: build low-cost houses on small infill plots in districts suffering the effects of sustained economic disinvestment and offer them for sale or rent. But it is a difficult idea to develop on a really large scale, not least because all infill sites have quite different characteristics – dimensions, topography, neighbours, subsoil conditions, local planning regulations … Nevertheless, at least two of Johnsen Schmaling's prototypical designs have been built (see Urban Infill 01, page 90).

It is more common for architects to double as developers. In this scenario the architect identifies the site and takes on all the pressure for a successful outcome. This often has the effect of streamlining the number of parties involved in the process – to save costs the architects can act as project managers, interior designers and estate agents – and creating a clarity of vision that all too often gets lost in the complex process of building on an infill site.

8 Spittelau Viaduct Housing (2006), Vienna, by Zaha Hadid Architects. The undulating design has created a sequence of indoor and outdoor spaces, the latter enlivened by the infill of bars and restaurants under the arches of the viaduct.

9 Urban Infill 02 (2007), the second low-cost infill designed and built by Johnsen Schmaling Architects in Milwaukee, Wisconsin.

10 Rag Flats, 'Fishtown', Philadelphia (2006), by Onion Flats with Minus Studios and Cover. This multi-unit housing scheme is built in and around a former factory.

Some architects have even become specialist designer–developers. Since the mid-1990s Jonathan Segal, a San Diego-based architect, has been the driving force behind the design and development of over 300 medium-to-high density urban residential, mixed-use and live/work units, many of them on former industrial and infill sites. Segal also runs

seminars and workshops advising other aspiring architect–developers. On the East Coast, architect brothers Tim and Patrick McDonald, along with friend Kurt Schlenbaker (all part of the Onion Flats development collective), have to date converted three run-down industrial sites into residential and mixed-use projects. The most recent, Rag Flats,

11 Haarlemmerbuurt (1995), Amsterdam, by Claus en Kaan Architecten. Part of a larger urban renewal scheme in the historic Haarlemmerstraat area, this three-apartment development joins an existing historic building to a new adjacent infill structure.

12

13

comprises 11 small flats on the site of a former fish storage depot in Philadelphia.

Developing an infill site is also an effective way for a young architectural practice to actually get something built. In Graz, Austria, a group of four young architects raised the finance to acquire a long-term infill site on the edge of the old city centre and built the Golden Nugget, a complex of apartments with a large ground-floor studio (see page 44). The sale of the apartments helped to fund the development, and the architects also got an office. Furthermore, the city of Graz benefited as the Golden Nugget has begun to change perceptions of a corner of the city centre that was suffering from a slightly negative reputation.

The revival of deprived areas and increased urban density are two of the many positive knock-on effects of infill housing. In many cases, empty sites and derelict buildings are found in less salubrious areas; perhaps places with lower socio-economic demographics, high unemployment or a reputation for crime. In these areas, land and housing stock are often affordable and planning constraints not too onerous. In some cases, local authorities actually offer incentives for the development of abandoned sites.

About this book

The following five chapters are arranged according to the nature of the sites upon which the houses are located. The challenge to owners of envisaging life in underground, partially submerged, steeply sloping or constrained mid-terrace sites, and then commissioning architects to realize their dreams seemed to us to be the primary common denominator behind these diverse and often extremely innovative projects.

<u>12</u> House and Atelier Bow-Wow (2006), Tokyo. The authors of *Pet Architecture* responded to the limitations of a difficult site by designing their own four-storey live/work premises with two sloping façades and a series of split-level floors.

<u>13</u> Ambi-Flux (2004), Tokyo, by Akira Yoneda. The multi-use steel-framed tower exemplifies the Japanese 'pet architecture' trend.

<u>14</u> Thin Wall House (2002), Tezuka Architects, Tokyo. The house maximizes interior volume with thin walls and the steepest permissible roof pitch.

There were other options available. When *Curious Footprints* was still the working title there was a proposal to arrange the projects according to the shapes of the sites, whether triangular, oblong or trapezoidal. Other possibilities were to arrange the projects typologically or geographically. We could also have filled the entire book with Japanese houses.

In recent years, Tokyo, in particular, has witnessed the construction of countless tiny, unconventional houses on awkward sites, many of them designed by young architects with an apparently boundless enthusiasm for novelty. Atelier Bow-Wow, a practice led by Yoshiharu Tsukamoto and Momoyo Kaijima, has even published a book about the phenomenon. *Pet Architecture*[2] documents houses, offices, restaurants, bars and even bike shops that have been squeezed into minuscule sites. It is a theme that is evident in their own work, such as the Mado Building, a house shaped like a cut diamond perched on a triangular traffic island, and House Tower, a five-storey reinforced-concrete dwelling with a footprint of only 18 square metres (194 square feet).

Other recent examples in *Pet Architecture* include a pencil-thin steel-framed tower between a café and a cycle repair shop designed by Akira Yoneda with Masahiro Ikeda. The lower two levels of 'Ambi-Flux' are for rent; the upper three comprise a self-contained town home complete with a roof garden.

Tezuka Architects' response to maximizing space on a small site in a dense residential neighbourhood was to design a house with the thinnest walls possible. It is composed of nine millimetre (0.35 inch) steel plates and 100mm × 100mm (4 inch × 4 inch) columns.

Confronted with an equally congested site, and planning guidelines limiting the number of windows permissible, TNA Architects designed Mosaic House, whose principal source of natural light is through the roof, resembling a flower stretching towards the sunlight.

The lengths to which site constraints are forcing architects all over the world to innovate in order to deliver basic requirements of domestic comfort – a sense of space, natural light and good ventilation – is extraordinary. But as the 40 houses covered in this book demonstrate, they are responding to the challenge, with great wit, sensitivity and invention.

[1] US Bureau of the Census, *Ranking Tables for Incorporated Places of 100,000 or More: Population in 2000, and Population Change from 1990 to 2000*, PHC-T-5.

[2] *Pet Architecture Guide Book*, Tokyo Institute of Technology, Tsukamoto Lab and Atelier Bow-Wow (World Photo Press, Japan 2002).

15 Billboard Building (2005), Tokyo, by Klein Dytham architecture. Only 2 metres (7 feet) wide by 11 metres (36 feet) long, the Billboard Building was constructed by a shipbuilding company and transported to site in five pieces. It was erected in half a day.

16 M – House (2006), Nagoya, by architectureW. The top-floor living area, cantilevered over the entry, is enclosed by sliding glass walls, opening the space up to the sun, cross ventilation and views.

16

302 STATION STREET

Melbourne, Australia
Architect Graeme Gunn Architects
Plot size 180m² / 1,938ft²

1 Four panels of operable steel louvres frame the first-floor window on the front façade. They mimic in dimension the neighbouring shutters of the Victorian cottages and protect the master bedroom from the harsh Australian sun.

2 Two dwellings on the site are connected by a shared courtyard. The bluestone crazy paving was inspired by the courtyard of eminent Australian architect Robin Boyd. A seat made of spotted gum runs along the southern wall and conceals six rainwater tanks that service the toilets and washing machine.

3 A balcony on the upper level of the house overlooks the main internal courtyard to the east.

3

The previous owner of 302 Station Street in the inner Melbourne suburb of North Carlton was a mysterious figure. When the derelict house went up for sale in 2003 it had been empty for 40 years. Unable to track down the owner, the local council was forced to foot the AUS$40,000 bill to demolish most of the single-storey Victorian house because it was deemed a safety hazard. Only the façade of the house and veranda were left standing, propped up with steel supports, when the new owners bought the property.

The design challenge presented to local practice Graeme Gunn Architects was to create a new building form that responded to the context of a site measuring 5 metres by 36 metres (16 feet by 118 feet): a row of Victorian single-storey structures on the north side; and five contemporary two- and three-storey town houses running along the southern boundary with their courtyards and terraces facing the infill site.

After protracted discussions with the local council and heritage advisers, the retained façade was

2

demolished and a new façade was designed to make a transition from 'old' to 'new'.

The result is two light-filled buildings placed around a central courtyard. The courtyard space also allows sunlight to penetrate the southern neighbours' back gardens. The front house contains an uninterrupted ground-floor living area, with two double bedrooms and two bathrooms on the first floor and a small unobtrusive laundry. The studio has private access off a rear laneway and includes a ground-floor living space with a small kitchen that can also function as a garage. The first floor has a generously sized bedroom and en-suite bathroom.

Integrated storage, including bookshelves and cupboards, was a central part of the design brief. Drawers beneath the staircase in the front house were inspired by thirteenth-century Japanese stairwell chests, and sliding drawers under the daybed in the upstairs bedroom are used to store shoes and linen.

Honey-hued American-oak floorboards line the ground-floor living space in the front house, and a polished concrete entry platform and exposed structural steel columns give the space a warehouse feel. Graeme Gunn has been designing since 1962 and his architecture has a refined, timeless quality. His signature colour is a steely blue-grey which is evident throughout the Station Street dwellings.

The exterior façade of the front house is rendered concrete. Four panels of steel louvres protrude from the first-floor window. They open and close electronically from a switch in the bedroom and provide shade from the harsh western sun during summer months. The local council insisted that the design of the louvres reference the dimensions of the Victorian-era shutters on neighbouring houses, creating a sympathetic transition from 'old' to 'new'.

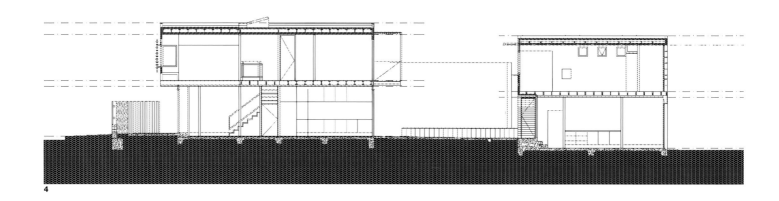

4

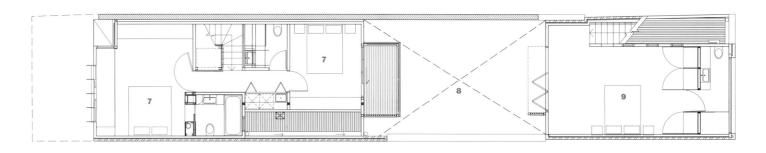

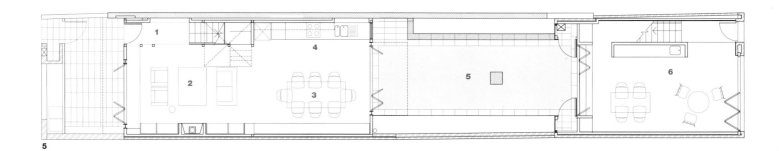

<u>4</u> Section.

<u>5</u> Ground- and first-floor plans. (1) entry, (2) living, (3) dining, (4) kitchen, (5) courtyard, (6) garage/ studio, (7) bedroom, (8) void over courtyard, (9) studio bedroom.

<u>6</u> The staircase is composed of four steel posts that support a continuous glass balustrade and the floor above.

<u>7</u> American-oak floorboards line the continuous ground-floor living room. A stainless-steel kitchen bench and exposed steel columns give the space a warehouse feel.

6

7

AAG HOUSE
Albuixech, Spain
Architect Manuel Cerdá Pérez & Julio Vila Liante – MCP Arquitectura
Building footprint 140m² / 1,507ft² approx

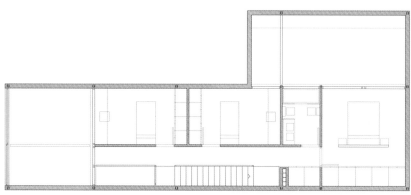

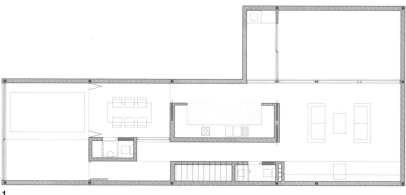

1

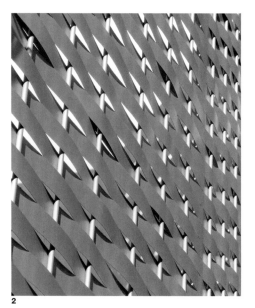

2

An enthusiasm for experimenting with materials and a respect for Mediterranean construction traditions are two of the defining features of this three-storey family house on a tight L-shaped plot in a small town on Spain's east coast.

Albuixech (population 3,500) is an unshowy kind of place about 15 kilometres (nine miles) north of Valencia, with much of its urban fabric dating from the early years of the twentieth century. The narrow, sunburned streets are full of utilitarian buildings composed of local materials and built by local labour. Calle Jesus, a street close to the town centre, is typical.

After years lying empty, the building that previously occupied 13 Calle Jesus – a structure almost identical to its neighbours – had fallen into dereliction. It was in this state that it was bought by a young couple who had recently become parents for the first time.

The couple knew up-and-coming Valencia architect Manuel Cerdá Pérez through a contractor friend; since setting up in practice in 1999 Pérez has developed a

reputation for an inventive approach to contemporary new-build residential architecture. So he was commissioned to design a replacement for the derelict building. The couple's instructions were: to build a house with a living room, dining space, three bedrooms, a courtyard, and perhaps a roof terrace.

Cerdá's solution was to position the body of the building in the centre of the plot, creating courtyards open to the elements at the front and rear. The idea, derived from local building traditions, was to harness the natural ventilation of the cool sea breezes to modulate the internal temperature: the rear courtyard, facing southeast, is warm; the north-facing courtyard is cooler.

To screen the front courtyard from the sun and noise of the street Cerdá took inspiration from Marcel Duchamp's 'ready made' sculptures, in which the French-born artist subverted perceptions of common objects – such as a urinal or a bicycle wheel – by rendering them as sculptural objects in unexpected

1 From bottom: ground and upper floor plans. The building is positioned in the centre of the L-shaped plot, creating space for external courtyards at either end.

2 The metal of the façade is typically used in the manufacture of garage doors.

3 The three-bedroom, three-storey infill replaces a derelict house that was built in the early twentieth century in the same materials and style as its two neighbours.

3

4

5

6

4 The linear arrangement of the ground floor extends from the dining area to the north to the courtyard at the rear.

5 On the upper level, the corridor extends onto an external balcony overlooking the front courtyard.

6 A steel staircase offers access to the roof terrace.

7 Entrance foyer: A pale colour scheme and extensive use of internal glazing maximize the sense of space in the narrow interior.

contexts. The metal strips that form the woven façade are typically used in garage doors. Cerdá used the metal on a much larger scale, and in an altogether more sophisticated manner. For him the experience was about: 'the possibilities of recycling … and giving a new image to a common, "dirty" material.'

The arrangement of the building itself is comparatively conventional. On the ground floor there is a sequence of dining room, galley kitchen and seating area, which opens on to the rear courtyard. On the upper level, a corridor links the three bedrooms – one double and two singles – and the large bathroom. At the north end a small external balcony overlooks the courtyard. Access to the gravel rooftop terrace is via a discreet steel staircase whose treads are embedded in the wall.

SÁNCHEZ MEDINA HOUSE
Toledo, Spain
Architect Manuel de las Casas
Building footprint 249m² / 2,680ft²

1 Southwest elevation, facing the Tagus Valley.

2 Section. An existing excavated area has been adapted as storage space.

3 Elevation. The roof slopes towards the courtyard.

4 Sánchez Medina House.

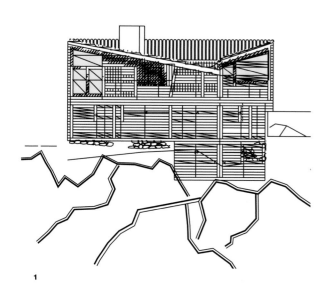

1

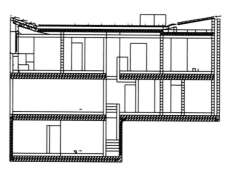

2

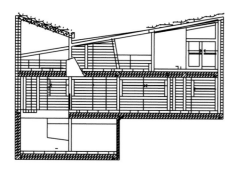

3

Opportunities to build in Toledo do not come around often. The historic Old City, perched on a mountain top and surrounded on three sides by the Tagus River, is a UNESCO World Heritage Site. Moorish, Christian and Jewish cultures stand side by side, a testament to centuries of religious tolerance. The consistency of forms and materials suggest a city in complete harmony with its environment, and with a strong sense of identity. It comes as no surprise to find that Toledo was once the capital of the Spanish Empire.

The cliff-edge plot for which architect Manuel de las Casas designed this five-bedroom family house was previously occupied by a partial ruin, the historical integrity of which had been compromised by a succession of alterations. The most recent phase of works had caused substantial sections of the walls to collapse; only the façades facing Calle Santa Ana and Plaza del Mirador had survived unscathed. To de las Casas the damage was a boon in his efforts to secure consent to demolish the existing structure and build a

4

5 Clay bricks and iroko screens on the exterior conform to the city's planning guidelines.

6 Timber slats screen views over the valley on the enclosed ground-level terrace.

7 The upper-level courtyard provides private external space and optimizes views over the Tagus Valley.

8 The house has three façades, two overlooking the streets and squares of Toledo, the third overlooking the valley to the southwest.

6

7

new house from the ground up.

The two-storey structure is essentially a traditional Toledo house finished to contemporary standards. The materials conform to the city's planning guidelines: the external walls are a combination of iroko screens and clay brick with edgings of coloured concrete. Tapered roll tiles are used on the roofs.

Another traditional feature is the enclosed courtyard on the upper level, which ensures that the house incorporates outdoor space despite the limitations of the 15.42 metre × 19.25 metre (50 × 63 foot) site. It also makes full use of the spectacular views over the Tagus towards Los Cigarrales.

The ground floor comprises a lobby, four bedrooms, a laundry, a long, narrow enclosed terrace and a garage. The upper floor, arranged around the courtyard, incorporates a living room, dining area, kitchen and the master bedroom. An existing excavated area, a legacy of the previous building, has been converted for use as storage space.

Timber flooring has been used throughout the interior, except in the bathrooms, where ceramic tiles are used for both paving and wall tiling.

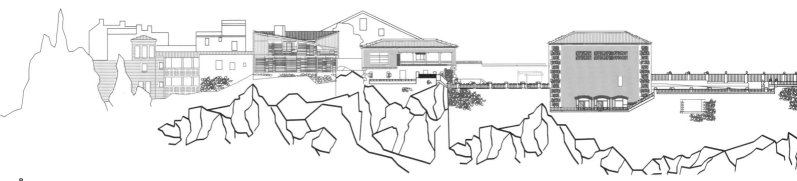

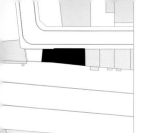

FAMILY HOUSE IN VICHY
Vichy, France
Architect Rémi Laporte
Building footprint 146m² / 1,572ft²

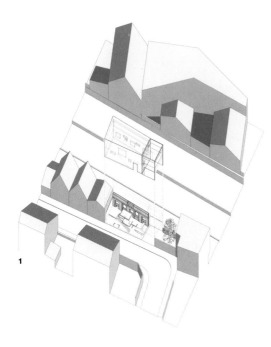

1

The young couple who commissioned architect Rémi Laporte to design this house for themselves and their two children had originally envisaged restoring an existing structure. Their attention turned to a new build because they could not find a building suited to their needs in a location close to Vichy town centre.

Apart from a determination not to contribute to edge-of-town urban sprawl, their other requirements for the future family home were for secure, private and adaptable dwelling with a minimal carbon footprint and strong connections to the exterior.

After an extensive search they settled on two small adjacent plots occupied by garages and a warehouse. This presented Laporte with a significant challenge. The existing buildings were not the issue as they had little architectural merit; the problem was that the plot was a flood-prone slither of land sandwiched between a road and a river. The diversity of neighbouring buildings was another hurdle: the north bank of the river is a heterogeneous residential area; the south side is light industrial.

Laporte's response was to position the compact, unpretentious two-storey volume in the widest part of the plot (6.5 metres / 21 feet), to maximize the footprint permitted under local planning regulations. He also inverted the traditional upstairs/downstairs domestic arrangement by placing the communal living areas on the upper level, to make the most of daylight and views over the river. The colour scheme of light grey paint and galvanized metal ensures that the building blends seamlessly with its neighbours.

The house is relatively lightweight and cost-effective. The hollow concrete blocks that make up the façades are vertical loadbearing walls. Only the cross-beams and framing are composed of structural metal; boards of untreated laminated spruce form the floor of the upper level; the sloping roof is made of sheet steel.

The cost savings made on the structure enabled Laporte to specify: an expansive aluminium-framed

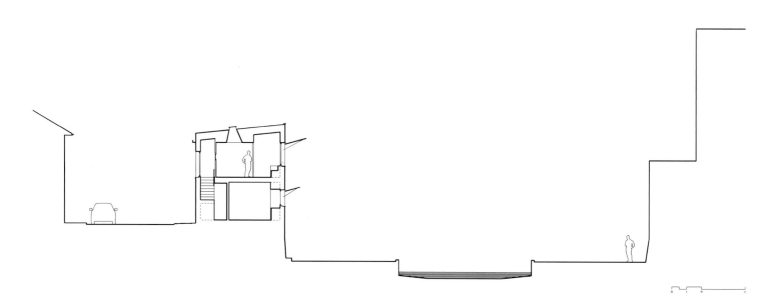

2

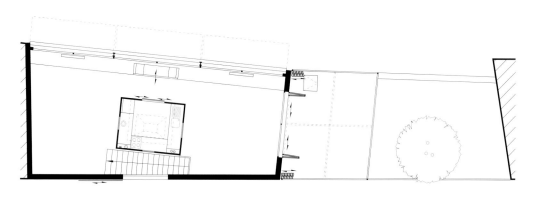

1 Axonometric emphasizing the complexities of the site, including a road and river, residential and industrial buildings.

2 Section from north to south.

3 From bottom: Ground- and first-floor plans. Bedrooms and bathrooms are on the ground level with the kitchen, living area and terrace on the upper level.

4 The composition of the southern façade expresses the internal layout of the building: three bedrooms on the ground floor and a large open-plan upper level.

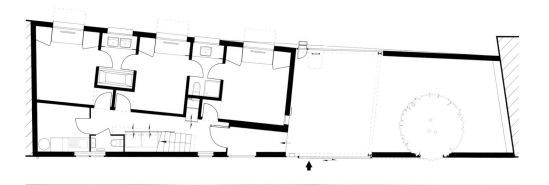

3

5

window opening on the upper level to optimize the south-facing river views; low emission glazing; thermodynamic heating (reversible air-conditioning); and reinforced insulation around the bedrooms. Another energy-conscious device was the insertion of a lined cavity on the southern façade to increase thermal efficiency. On the lower level this layer doubles as bedroom storage and desk space; upstairs it forms an integrated bench and kitchen storage.

The building is entered from the road via a sliding gate. An entrance lobby leads into a red-painted corridor, which connects the three ground-level bedrooms and bathrooms. A staircase leads to the upstairs living space, which is a single open-plan space divided by a kitchen in the middle. At the west end of the building the upper level extends onto a terrace with a lightweight steel pergola. Over time a canopy of honeysuckle will enclose the space.

5 On the northern façade a metal screen and sliding gate shield the house and hard-landscaped parking area from the street.

6 A lined cavity on the southern façade increases thermal efficiency as well as providing bedroom storage and desk space.

7 A kitchen block in the centre of the upper level divides the otherwise open-plan communal living area.

6

7

8 The entrance foyer offers access to the three ground-floor bedrooms and the staircase.

9 The communal living areas are placed on the upper level to make the most of daylight and views over the river.

10 Over time a canopy of honeysuckle will enclose the pergola on the terrace.

9

10

FORT GREENE HOUSE
Brooklyn, New York, USA
Architect Christoff:Finio Architecture
Building footprint 144m² / 1,550ft²

1 Section. Clients, Darcy Miro and Lars Weiss, had very specific ideas about how they wanted the new building to function, both as a home and a studio for their separate businesses as a jewellery maker and music producer.

2 West garden elevation. Rather than using standard residential windows, the architects suggested using industrial storefront windows. The aluminium castings suit the industrial finishes in the house.

3 Sympathetically contemporary, the new town house is noticeably different but adds to, rather than detracts from, the neighbourhood's historic character.

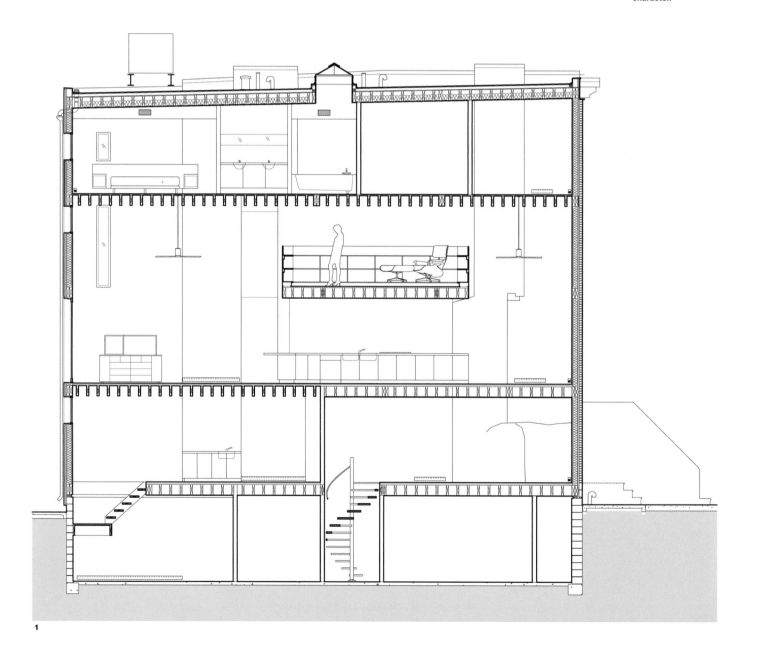

1

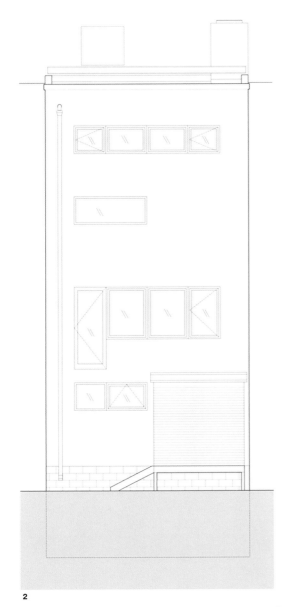

2

3

When Darcy Miro and her husband, Lars Weiss, chanced upon a derelict site in the heart of Brooklyn, they immediately saw the opportunity to build their own home.

The couple were renting a studio nearby in the Brooklyn neighbourhood of Fort Greene and had been eyeing the 6 x 24 metre (20 x 79 foot) plot for more than a year before they seriously looked into buying it. They discovered that the city council had demolished the old town house in 1993 and the owner was eager to sell the remaining land. They bought the site shortly afterwards for US$180,000.

Miro, a jewellery designer, and Weiss, a music producer, had very specific ideas about how they wanted the new building to function, both as a home and a studio for their separate businesses. They approached architect Martin Finio who had recently launched his own practice, Christoff:Finio Architecture, with wife Taryn Christoff. The architects were commissioned on the basis that they would design the

shell and the clients would be responsible for the details and finishes.

The result is a sympathetically contemporary four-storey town house with basement that replicates the form and height of the neighbouring town houses. The site is defined by the walls shared with the two existing adjacent properties. Rather than frame, insulate and clad these walls, Miro and Weiss were determined to leave the surfaces exposed, incorporating them into the interior of the new building.

The sleeping quarters (three bedrooms) and two bathrooms are on the top floor; below is a loft-like reading room where their young son has plenty of space to play. This mezzanine overlooks the double-height living and dining room on the first floor. The ground floor and basement are dedicated to the couple's professions – a jewellery workshop and a recording studio.

Throughout the house Miro and Weiss have used concrete and wood plank flooring and have left many

of the ducts, pipes and electrical conduits exposed. It was a labour of love for the couple, who began construction in 2002. It took much longer to finish than anticipated, with the house finally ready in 2004.

4 From left: Plans of the
ground, first and second
floors.

5 Double-height ceilings
in the living room create a
sense of space.

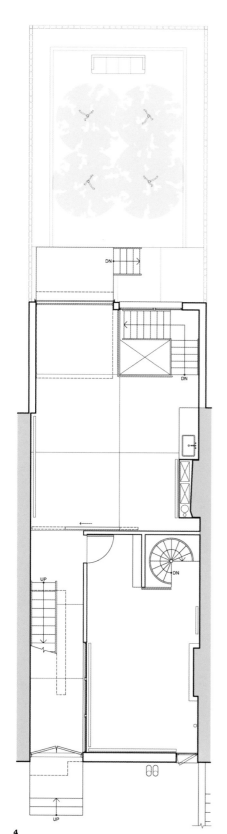

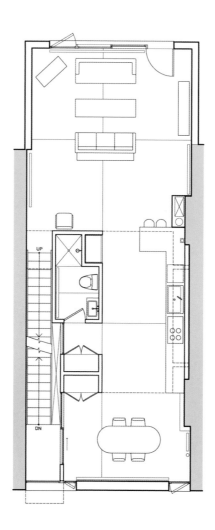

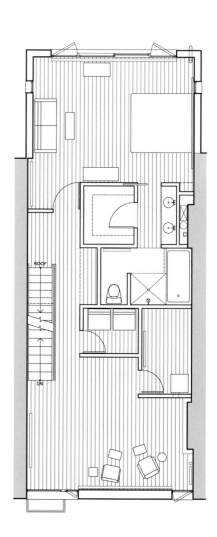

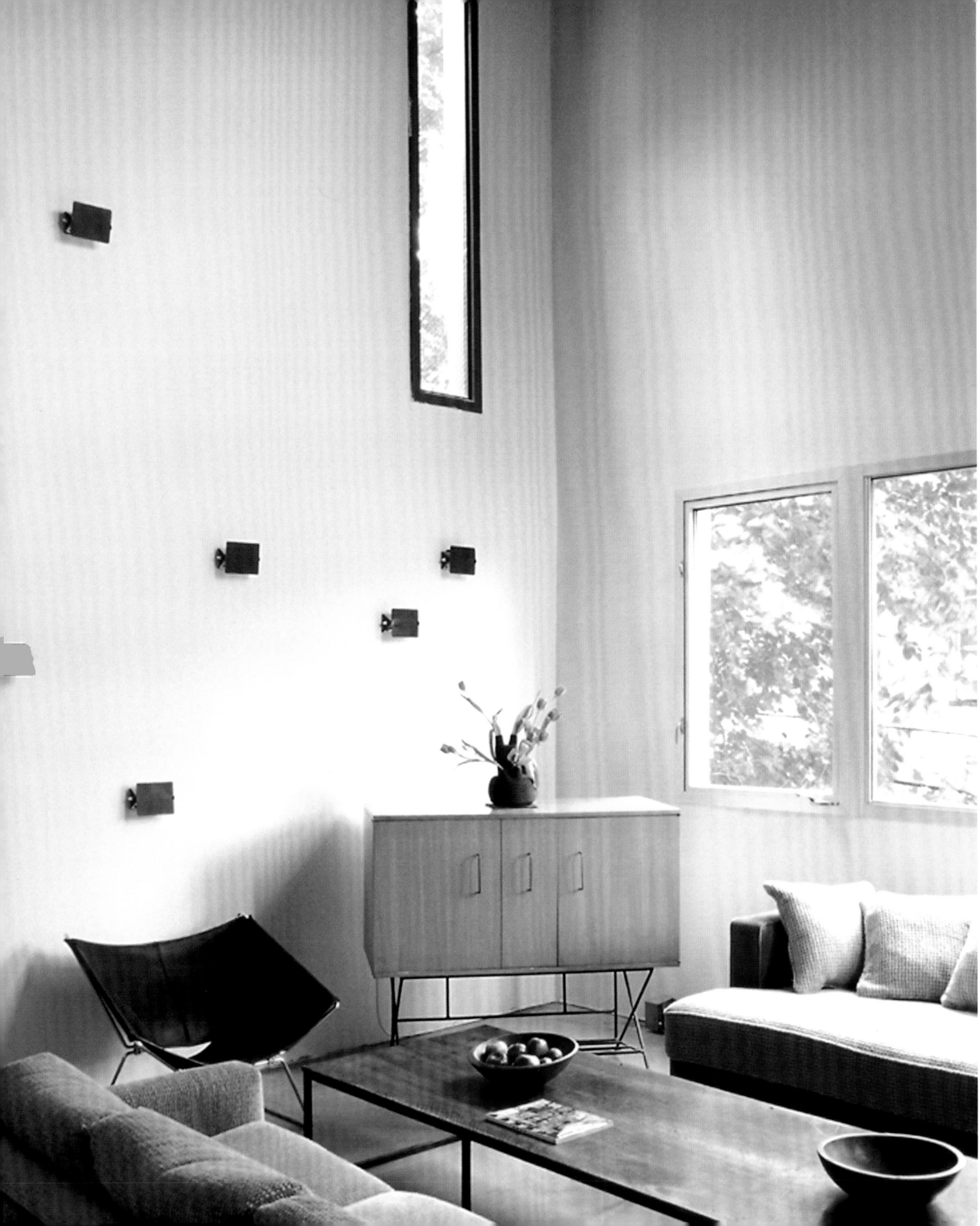

6 A staircase runs alongside the exterior walls of the neighbouring building which the clients intentionally left exposed as a reminder of the history of their site.

7 The couple's reading room is technically a first-floor mezzanine that overlooks the central living space below.

8 Inexpensive aluminum-magnesium 'speed rails' were specified for the banisters and railings around the reading loft, giving the space an industrial aesthetic.

7

8

GOLDEN NUGGET
Graz, Austria
Architect INNOCAD
Site area 297m² / 3,197ft²; building footprint: 197m² / 2,120ft²

1 The six-storey infill tapers at the top, creating the missing middle step between the roof heights of the adjacent town houses.

2 Rear elevation.

3 Section. The upper levels are private apartments, with office space on the ground floor and part of the first floor.

2

The Golden Nugget, in the centre of Graz, comprises office space and five well-appointed apartments. It was developed, designed and marketed by a group of four young Austrian architects. Their inventive and open-minded approach to the challenge was fundamental to the revival of a site that had been underachieving for decades.

Prior to its redevelopment, 65 Grazbachgasse was home to an unremarkable single-storey shop selling kitchen equipment, and a redundant residential building dating from the eighteenth century. For years, developers had explored ways of reviving the trapezoidal plot, but without success. There were two notable obstacles.

Firstly, the parcel of land is sandwiched between two historic town houses only 50 metres (164 feet) from the historic centre of Graz, which is a UNESCO-designated World Heritage Site. This means that development constraints are severe: any new building proposed for the site had to be submitted to a

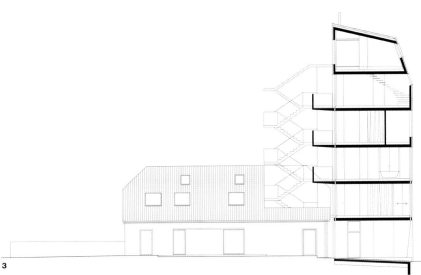

3

4

5

6

4 The site is only 50 metres (164 feet) from the historic centre of Graz, a UNESCO World Heritage Site. The architects managed to convince the planning authorities that the colour and form of the Golden Nugget complements the Wilhelminian style of the surrounding buildings.

5 A heritage protected two-storey building in the rear courtyard has been integrated into the Golden Nugget.

6 The gold finish and arrangement of window openings are departures from buildings in the immediate vicinity.

7 Anticlockwise from left: ground-, second-, third-, fourth- and fifth-floor plans.

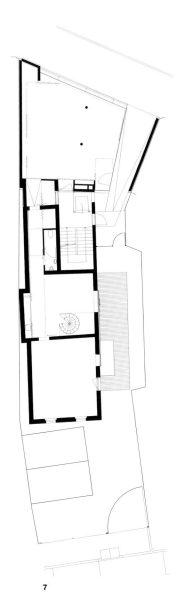

7

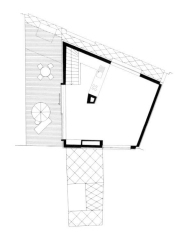

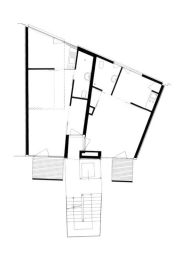

committee of experts. The second problem was the existing two-storey residential building, which is a protected historic structure. Failure to integrate it into any new development would have meant forfeiting building rights. The combination of stringent planning guidelines and heritage constraints rendered conventional development proposals economically unviable. Innovative thinking was needed.

Martin Lesjak, Andreas Reiter, Peter Schwaiger and Bernd Steinhuber – the four INNOCAD partners – decided to take on the financial risk of developing the site as well as negotiating the planning hurdles to design the new building for it. This streamlined approach engendered a clarity of vision that might have been lacking in a partnership between funding bodies, project managers, architects, estate agents and so on. The five apartments sold off-plan, providing a financial base for the project. The architects themselves decided to use part of the building as their office.

The existing building in the courtyard and the ground floor of the new six-storey structure comprises office space for INNOCAD, and its sister company 99 PLUS, Project and Property Development. Apartments of varying specifications occupy the upper levels.

The new building has a concrete frame consisting of two fireproof walls, two central columns and concrete floor slabs. The non-loadbearing exterior walls are timber framed.

Its street-facing façade re-establishes the form of the historic streetscape; the top floor tapers back to create the middle step between the roof heights of the adjacent structures. However, the extent of glazing, form of the window openings and colour of the façade are notable departures.

INNOCAD was able to convince the committee of experts that gold matches the surrounding Wilhelminian buildings, and connects the different building styles in the vicinity. Gold is also the colour of INNOCAD's corporate identity.

The theme carries through into the interiors. The walls of the ground-floor offices are gold, as are curtains in the flats above, although to make a distinction between the ages of the buildings the interior of the refurbished courtyard building is white.

Since the building was completed it has become a notable local landmark. It has also acted as a catalyst for the development of the area.

8 The five apartments sold off-plan, providing a source of financial security for the development.

9 & 10 The two-storey building at the rear of the site has been converted into two levels of office space for **INNOCAD** and its sister company **99 PLUS**.

11 INNOCAD's ground-floor office is a prominent 'shop window' for the young practice.

10

9

11

DRYER HOUSE
Baden, Austria
Architect BKK-3
Site area 513m² / 5,522ft²; house footprint: 178m² / 1,916ft²

1 Sections through the longer north wing. The front of the house is on the right, and the rear on the left. Storage space and a studio are incorporated in the basement.

2 Plans of the ground and first floors. (1) entrance, (2) garage, (3) kitchen, (4) multi-use space, (5) living area, (6) garden, (7) bridge, (8) bedroom, (9) atrium.

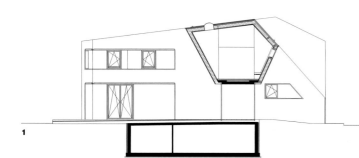

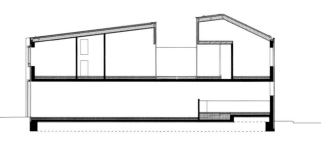

1

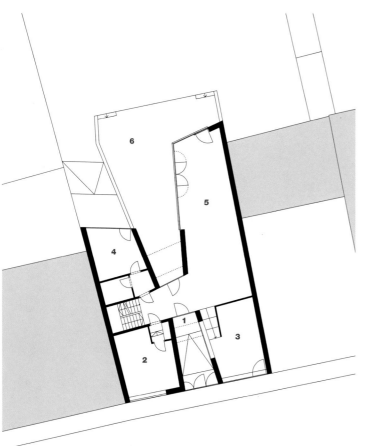

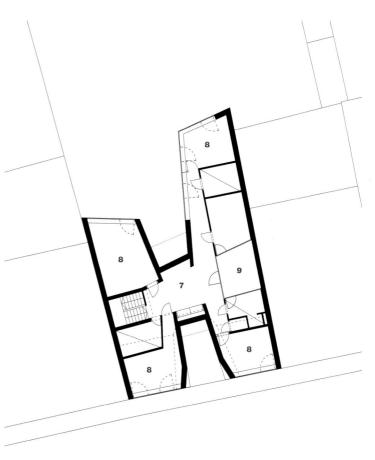

2

3 BKK-3's reinterpretation of the conventional edge-of-block two-storey family home was inspired by the Paarhof, a traditional farmhouse with two buildings on either side of a courtyard.

'We want to have a path running right through the house,' said Mr and Mrs Dreier (the title of the house is a pun on their name). It was a request that initiated a design process that lasted several years.

BKK-3's clients had bought a narrow site in Baden, a picturesque spa town 25 kilometres (16 miles) south of Vienna that has become increasingly popular with young families escaping the pace of life in the capital. The plot was narrow – it had previously been a garden – and bordered on both sides by residential buildings. It was too difficult to incorporate a path along either side without eating into precious space, so it was decided to construct the building around a central pathway. To reinforce the intent, the same paving slabs were used outside and inside the building.

The pathway divides the building into two wings, connected on the first floor by a 'bridge'. This arrangement is expressed on the front façade by the recessed entrance. To allow daylight to penetrate into the entrance recess, the passageway widens as it

4

5

extends upwards. As a consequence the roof of the building appears to reach almost to the ground.

There is a similar arrangement at the rear, where the house looks over a paved courtyard and garden. One notable difference is that the central bridge tilts out at an angle, creating a partially sheltered terrace below.

Slicing the building in two means that the two large rooms at the rear overlook the courtyard. Even at the front, where privacy is a consideration, the main rooms are flooded with natural light.

The internal arrangement of the house responds to the needs of the young family. The ground floor includes a garage, kitchen and large living area in a rear wing that reaches into the garden. The shorter wing opposite is multi-use space that can be used as a stand-alone apartment. On the first floor, BKK-3 incorporated three children's bedrooms, a master bedroom and two bathrooms. There is also an atrium, accessible from the bridge, one of the children's bedrooms and a bathroom.

One of the reasons that the design process took a few years was that the clients imposed no time pressure on BKK-3; they were more concerned with achieving the desired outcome than rushing things. Another issue was that the house lies in a conservation zone, which required close collaboration with the authorities. In this context it was an advantage that the basic form of the property was inspired by the Paarhof, a traditional Austrian farmhouse with gabled rear roofs, and street fronts of alternating gables and eaves. Paarhofs are also characterized by two buildings on either side of a courtyard.

<u>4</u> The uniform mint green colour of the walls and roof unites the fragmented volume.

<u>5</u> The width of the entrance recess increases at the first-floor level to allow light into the passageway.

<u>6</u> The building's catamaran-like footprint evolved from the clients' request to a have a path through the building.

<u>7</u> At the rear the house overlooks a garden and paved courtyard.

<u>8</u> The atrium on the upper level is accessible from the 'bridge', a bathroom and one of the bedrooms.

<u>9</u> The 'bridge' that connects the two wings is a space for quiet contemplation.

7

8

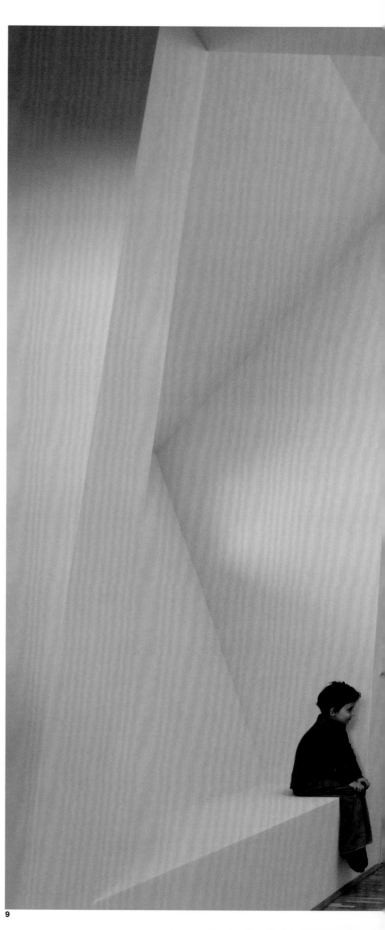

9

TOWN HOUSE
Tübingen, Germany
Architect KRISCHPARTNER
Plot size 71.5m² / 774ft²; 200m² / 2,153ft² of habitable space

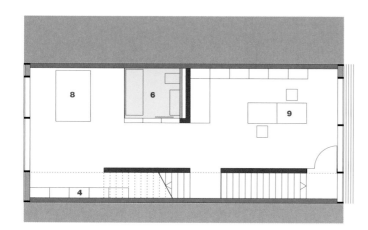

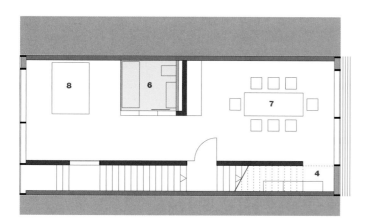

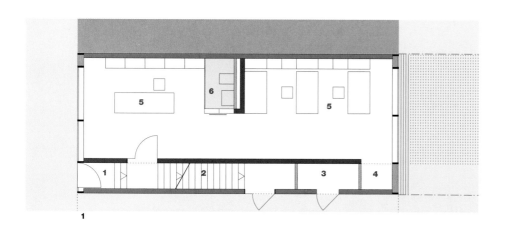

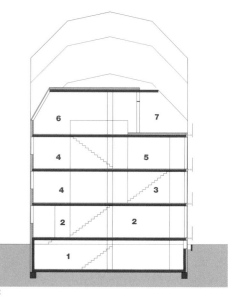

2

Tübingen, a university town in southwestern Germany, is unique not only for its historic character but also for its innovative new residential district that is helping to meet the town's housing shortages.

This four-storey town house sits between the firewalls of two adjacent buildings on a 5.5 metre (18 foot) wide site in the Südstadt, a former military barracks which has been developed into a new residential quarter with over 1,100 units.

Accommodating around 200 square metres (2,153 square feet) of usable floor space, the site is the smallest in the area. It was 'allocated' to the client as part of an innovative development process in which land is acquired and assembled by the municipality and then sold to building partnerships who commission an architect and a contractor to design and build their homes.

In this case local architect Rüdiger Krisch was also the client. Krisch's ambition was to construct an

1 From bottom: Plans of the ground, second and third floors. (1) entrance, (2) stair to basement, (3) refuse, (4) closet, (5) office, (6) bathroom, (7) kitchen/dining, (8) bedroom, (9) study.

2 Section. (1) basement, (2) office, (3) kitchen/dining, (4) bedroom, (5) study, (6) kitchen/dining/living, (7) roof terrace.

3 According to the regu– lations of the municipality, the building fronts directly onto the street in line with adjacent town houses. The position and height of the frontages is also in line with municipal regulations.

4 The southern façade is almost fully glazed to maximize solar gain.

5 Semi-private gardens and courtyards are an important feature of the new residential quarter.

affordable building that would have a flexible floor plan for multiple uses. The front is aligned with the perimeter of the block in order to adhere to the guidelines set down in the design code for the district, and the depth of all buildings on the block is the same (13 metres / 43 feet), as dicated by the zoning code. The height and architectural style for each new building on the block varies.

Krisch set back the top floor penthouse and created a large terrace. The southern façade looks out over a semi-private grassed courtyard and is almost completely glazed, maximizing solar energy gain. The northern exterior faces directly onto the street and consists of fibre cement panels, smaller windows and a sloping glazed roof.

A stairwell along the western party wall allows for efficient circulation and each floor has an open-plan warehouse feel that can accommodate domestic as well as commercial uses. Krisch lives on the top two floors and rents the ground and first floors as an artist's studio and accommodation. The top floor has a generous kitchen and living space which steps out onto the timber deck. Internally the party walls towards the neighbouring buildings are white; the rest of the walls and ceilings are exposed concrete with orange brick terrazzo floors.

7

6 The interior is defined by a palette of whitewashed walls, exposed concrete ceilings and rich orange terrazzo floors.

7 The top-floor living space opens out through bifold doors to a roof terrace.

8 Views of the surrounding terraces through the glazed sloping roof in the kitchen.

8

STAIRCASE HOUSE
Barcelona, Spain
Architect exe.arquitectura
Plot size 110m² approx / 1,184ft² approx

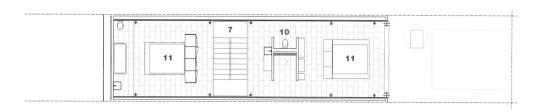

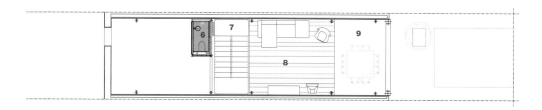

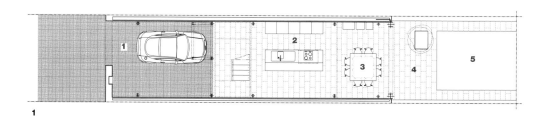

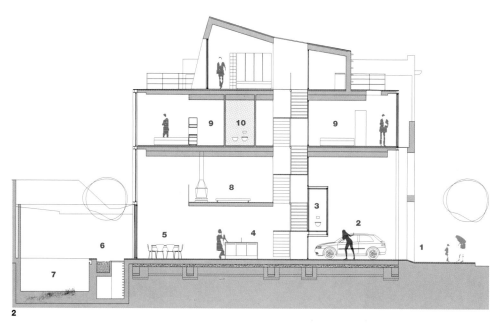

The suspended staircase that gives this narrow house its name both unites and divides the three-storey structure. It offers access to the two upper levels and mezzanine, while simultaneously suggesting boundaries between rooms in a house designed without internal doors. The thin traction wires that support the staircase also allow light to permeate from the large rooflight above throughout the interior spaces below. The overall effect could hardly be more different from the house that previously occupied the site.

The house occupies the footprint of a *casa de cos* (which translates loosely as 'fits like a glove'), a nineteenth-century Catalan house type defined by a long, narrow plot in a dense neighbourhood. Built in 1813, the *casa* had undergone some modifications over the years, including the addition of a new façade in 1897, and had spent the last 30 years of its life as a bar. By the late 1990s the structure was seriously dilapidated. It was demolished shortly afterwards with only the limestone façade being retained.

1 From bottom: Ground-floor, first-floor mezzanine and first-floor plans. (1) entry courtyard, (2) kitchen, (3) dining, (4) terrace, (5) pool, (6) toilet, (7) staircase, (8) mezzanine living room, (9) void over dining room, (10) bathroom, (11) bedroom. The new house sits in the centre of the long narrow footprint. A garage occupies the front 4 metres (13 feet); a paved patio and lap pool are situated at the rear.

2 Section. (1) street, (2) entrance courtyard, (3) toilet, (4) kitchen, (5) dining room, (6) terrace, (7) pool, (8) mezzanine living room, (9) bedroom, (10) bathroom.

3 The door of the limestone façade, the only surviving feature of the original building, was widened to allow a car inside.

The challenge facing Barcelona practice exe.arquitectura was to design a new house suited to twenty-first-century metropolitan lifestyles between the existing party walls. Light, flexibility and spatial continuity were among the client's specifications. It was from this brief that architects Marc Obrado Cebada and Elisabeth Sadurní Moreta developed the concept for the suspended staircase. But that was not where the innovation ended.

Viewed from the street little appears to have changed. The architects' only alteration was to widen the doorway to accommodate a car. It is only from inside the garage that the 'secondary façade' of steel and glass becomes apparent.

A door offers access to the open-plan kitchen and dining area, which in turn opens onto the south-facing patio and lap pool at the rear. Full-height doors across the width of the opening create a sense of continuity between the exterior and interior, a sense reinforced by the use of grey slate pavers across both areas.

3

4

The first room on the ascent up the staircase is a guest bathroom, enclosed in chipboard, which projects out into the garage. A further half-flight leads to a carpeted seating area accommodated on a mezzanine in the void above the kitchen/dining area, which is illuminated by the glazed rear façade.

Two bedrooms occupy the first floor proper, divided by the staircase and a bathroom. The top floor accommodates a study and a service/storage area, with a small south-facing roof terrace. None of the rooms has a door; screens and strategically positioned partition walls provide privacy where required.

5

4 The garage acts as a cushion between the street and the 'secondary façade' of glass and steel.

5 To allow natural light into the centre of the building and to achieve spatial fluidity there are no doors inside the building. Instead the staircase acts as a 'horizontal filter'.

6 The staircase, the device that both unites and divides the house, is suspended on slender traction wires and anchored by girders attached to the walls.

7 Wedged between party walls, the Staircase House has no side windows. The interior is flooded with natural light by the glazed south-facing façade and a 2m × 5m (7ft × 15ft) skylight above the suspended staircase.

8 & 9 Full-height doors open the full width of the building to connect the kitchen/dining room to the rear patio and lap pool.

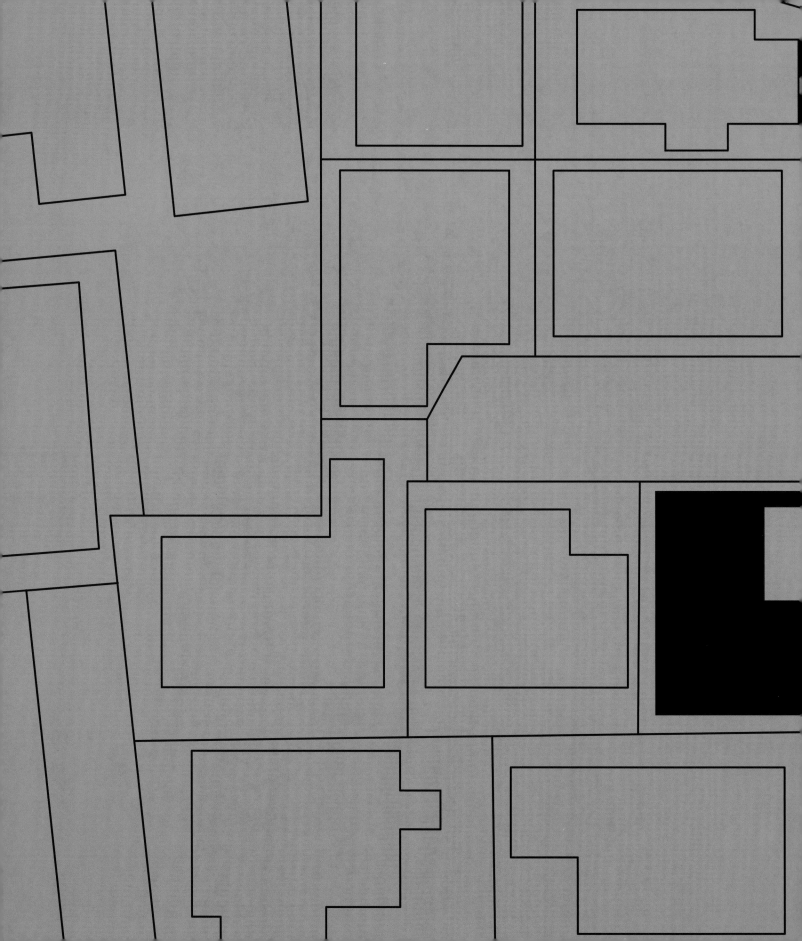

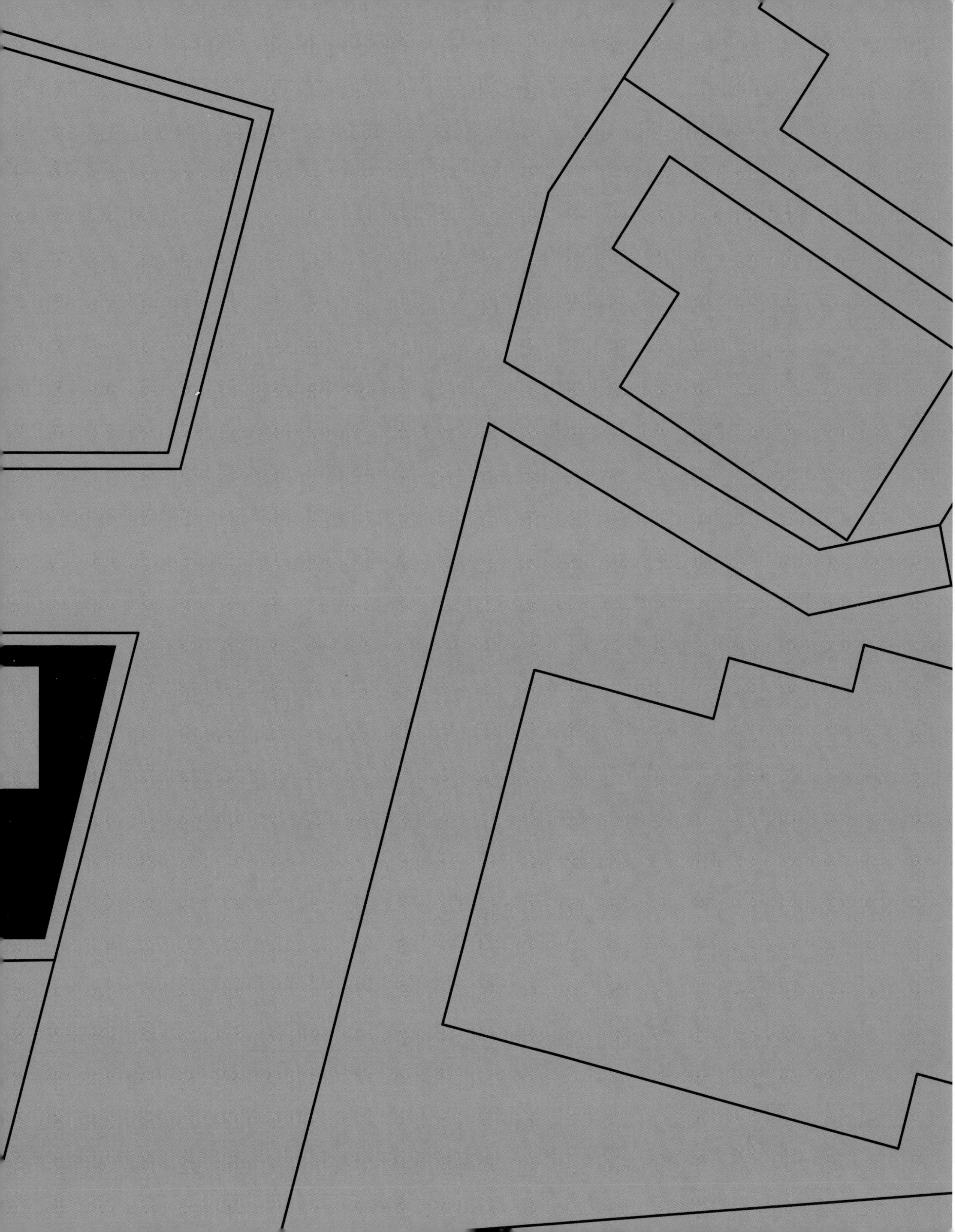

2 CORNER & END-OF-TERRACE PLOTS

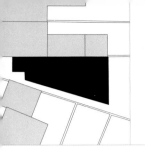

FOCUS HOUSE
London, UK
Architect bere:architects
Building footprint 70m² / 753ft²; site area: 174m² / 1,873ft²

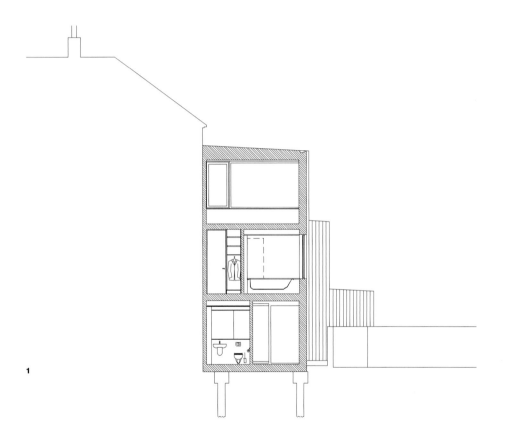

1

Compared to its tall, brick-built Victorian neighbours, Focus House in north London is a dynamic, zinc-sheathed flash of a building. It is also an exemplar of environmentally responsible, low impact twenty-first-century construction.

bere:architects' client bought the small triangular parcel of land and adjacent Victorian town house in 2004. His plan was to live in the latter while building a new house on the former. Justin Bere's brief was to design a flexible, low-cost, low-maintenance property with a minimal carbon footprint.

The ground floor tapers from a width of seven metres (23 feet) at the rear to three metres (ten feet) on the west-facing street façade. It includes an open-plan ground floor with living areas suited to the requirements of a family of five. At the back, sliding doors lead into a small paved garden, which includes a second low-slung structure for study and recreation.

The first floor of Focus House comprises two bedrooms and a bathroom, all connected by a

2

1 Section looking west. The street-facing façade is only 3 metres (10 feet) wide.

2 South elevation.

3 In appearance, environmental performance and internal layout, Focus House is a world away from its Victorian neighbour.

4 The triangular site determined the shape of the house: in order to secure planning permission, the new house could not exceed the profile of its neighbours.

4

corridor. The top storey includes the master bedroom and a study, which juts out over the front entrance. Storage space is built into the structure on every level, maximizing the available living area.

The walls, floors and roof slabs consist of cross-laminated timber imported from Austria and used in kit form. The slabs can span long distances and be erected quickly and with minimal on-site labour. Focus House was completed from start on site to full fit-out in only six months.

Foamglass was applied in sheets over the timber, creating a thick layer of insulation and an impermeable vapour barrier. A zinc skin covers the Foamglas, creating a durable exterior.

The house is sufficiently airtight and well insulated to require only minimal heating – heat recovery ventilation is used throughout. Solar thermal installation means that the house generates around 50 per cent of its annual hot water requirements.

Focus House won bere:architects the Royal Institute of British Architects Small House of the Year award (2007), and the Grand Designs Awards 'Best Eco House' (2007).

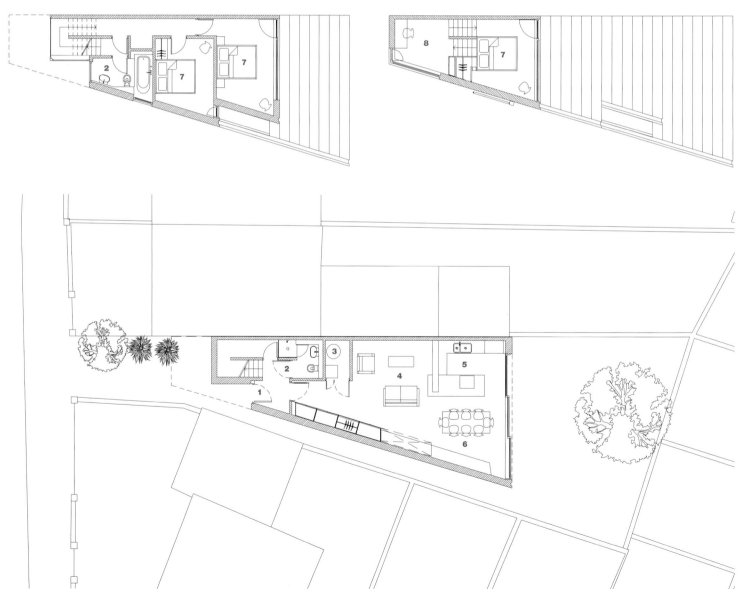

5 Clockwise from bottom: Ground-, first- and second-floor plans. (1) entrance, (2) bathroom, (3) utility room, (4) living area, (5) kitchen, (6) dining area, (7) bedroom, (8) study.

6 Rear elevation. The use of a timber superstructure meant that construction took only six months, and the building has very low levels of embodied energy.

7 View from the top-floor master bedroom towards the study; storage is built in throughout, to maximize living space.

8 Full-height sliding doors separate the kitchen from the paved garden at the rear. The living area has an oak floor, and rosewood fittings.

6

7

8

DUONG HOUSE
Lyons, France
Architect Philippe Villien
Plot size 116m² / 1,249ft² approx (footprint of restaurant)
300m² / 3,229ft² approx (total area of site)

1 The five-storey family house above a restaurant fills the gap between an alley and a nineteenth-century town house.

2 A recessed terrace resembling an open book aligns the front façade with the neighbouring building on the other side of the alley.

3 Philippe Villien's sketch of the corner infill.

4 Long and short sections.

2

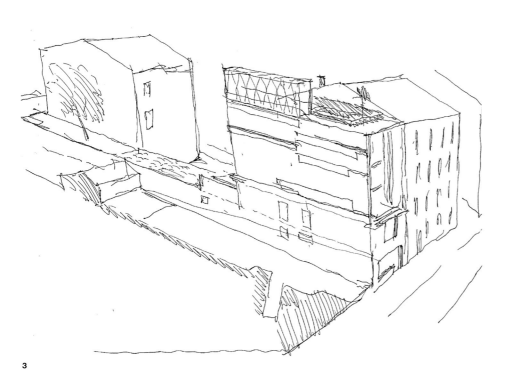

Vacant plots come in all shapes and sizes, typically in difficult-to-build-on, awkward-to-access locations with limited daylight and heritage constraints. In many cases an experienced eye is required to identify a plot, let alone develop it. That was certainly the case for this five-storey family house, which sits on top of a restaurant in Lyons' former silk weaving district.

The restaurant occupies a long, narrow plot adjacent to a pedestrian path at an angle of approximately 45 degrees to the grand tree-lined Boulevard de la Croix-Rousse. A pitched-roof town house sits on the opposite corner of the entrance to the alley. The challenge to the architect was to restore and refurbish the restaurant, and build a large private house on top of it. The clients, Dr and Mrs Duong, specified that their home was to include an open-air terrace, two living rooms (one double height), four bedrooms, three bathrooms, a kitchen and a laundry.

Understandably, the process of securing planning consent for the four metre (13 foot) wide rooftop

3

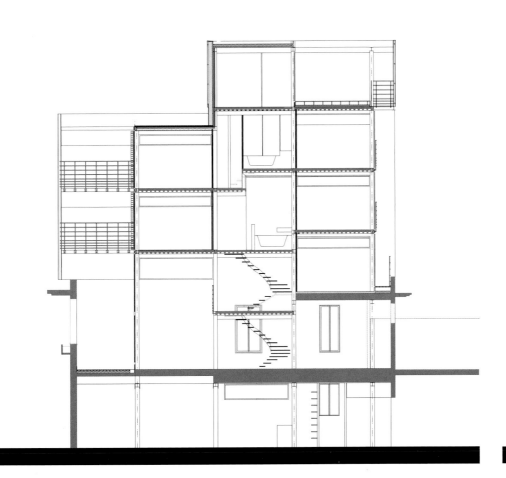

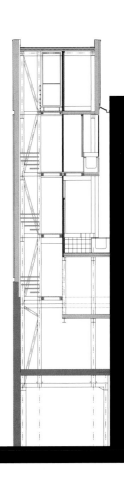

4

addition required time and perseverance. Bâtiments de France, the body that oversees the protection of historic monuments in France, rejected Villien's first proposal as too high; his second was thrown out because the roof terrace overlooked the boulevard. For these reasons, the third iteration – what we see today – had an introverted terrace 18 metres (59 feet) above ground level, and a top storey set back from the boulevard-facing façade.

The Duong's house is a distinctly contemporary presence in the nineteenth-century streetscape. Its front and rear façades are extensively glazed, and the alley-facing wall is wrapped in an envelope of translucent polycarbonate panels. This long side wall extends beyond the front of the building – which faces the street at 45 degrees in line with the alley – to create an upper façade in the form of an open book, a distinctive feature which also ensures that the building aligns with its neighbour.

Internally the house is arranged around a beautiful staircase of steel and rosewood, which rises elegantly through the centre of the building, linking together the numerous mezzanine levels, designed to make maximum use of the available space, and provide a fluid sense of ascension through the building. Effective use of space was such a paramount concern that on the upper levels the staircase risers double as drawers.

Twenty-five per cent of the materials in the building, including the staircase, balustrades and blinds, were sourced from Vietnam, the country of Dr and Mrs Duong's birth; the couple met in France, having fled their homeland during the 1980s. This had the combined effect of a substantial cost reduction – Philippe Villien estimates that he saved 25,000 euros on the staircase alone – and the creation of a house with a dual Franco-Asian character.

5 Boulevard (front) elevation.

6 The rosewood and steel staircase was handmade in Ho Chi Minh, Vietnam, a decision that saved over 25,000 euros and contributed to the distinct Franco-Asian character of the building's interior.

ONE WINDOW HOUSE
Venice, California, USA
Architect Touraine Richmond Architects
Plot size 138m² / 1,485ft²

1 The corrugated metal-clad box provides privacy for the sleeping zones on the first floor.

2 Section. The upper levels are the sleeping quarters with kitchen and living space on the ground floor.

3 Street elevation. The new house is on the left connected to the old house via a 3 metre (10 foot) wide platform.

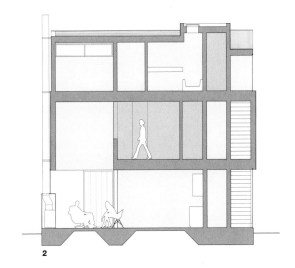

2

The popular residential neighbourhood of Venice, Los Angeles, has long been a hotbed of experimental architecture. Some of Frank Gehry's more progressive early buildings were in Venice, several of them sheathed in sheets of corrugated sheet steel, a material that dominates the exterior of this small family home on one half of a tight corner plot.

When architect couple Deborah Richmond and Olivier Touraine bought the site in 2002 it contained a two-storey stucco house dating from 1953. Their intention was to use it as an office and rental apartment and build a second dwelling for themselves next door. Unlike many developers they did not want to build to the perimeter of the site, preferring to build to the maximum height permitted (9 metres / 30 feet). This left space at the front of their property for an outdoor garden with native planting behind a timber fence.

The couple clad the first floor in corrugated steel so that from the street it would be impossible to see into the upper living and sleeping spaces, in contrast to the highly public ground floor. Known locally as the 'One Window House' there is only one traditional window, located in the top-floor bedroom, which provides natural ventilation. There are two skylights on the first floor, and the ground-floor kitchen and living area spills out through floor-to-ceiling glass doors onto a deck which compensates for the unbroken façade above.

Another regulatory hurdle influencing the design of the home was that it could have required additional car parking spaces. The couple decided to insert a three metre (ten foot) wide platform connecting the new house with the 1950s property. This 'connection' allows the buildings to be considered as a 'duplex' under local planning law, which meant a reduction in the provision of off-street car parking from six to five vehicles: two cars can fit under the 'platform' with another behind and two additional angled parking spaces are located adjacent to the old house.

Richmond and Touraine used unconventional materials to furnish the interior of their home. An engineered wood that is similar to, though more textured than, plywood lines the kitchen cabinets and stair treads. A red translucent curtain is used in place of a closet door and the premanufactured non-flammable fireplace box is mounted in a black material made of recycled pressed paper.

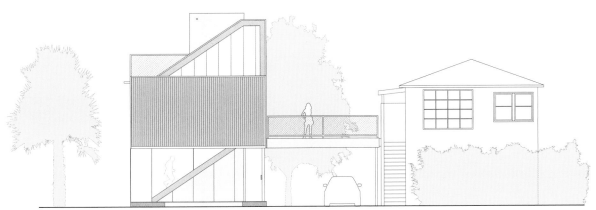

3

4

4 The angled roofline is designed to meet height restrictions in the neighbourhood.

5 From left: Ground-, first- and second-floor plans. (1) entrance, (2) living/dining/kitchen, (3) covered parking, (4) existing family dwelling, (5) study loft, (6) child's room, (7) void over living area, (8) roof deck, (9) master bedroom.

6 The house is set back from the plot line, enabling the architects to include a small garden and timber deck on the small site.

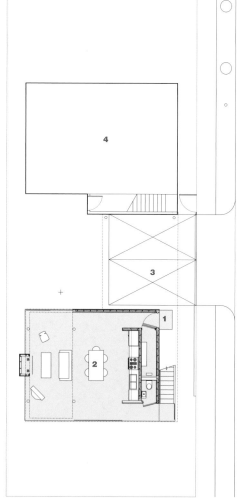

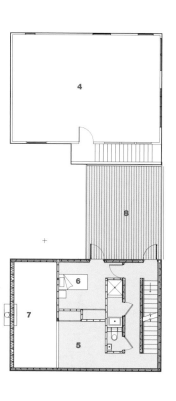

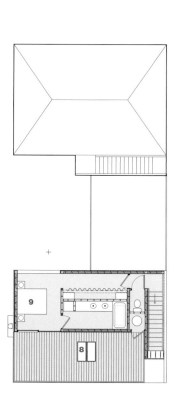

5

8

7 The interior spaces have been kept minimal, allowing the outside to blend seamlessly with the inside.

8 In the bedroom clothing is stored behind a red translucent curtain.

9 The small bedroom opens out onto a timber deck with a chain link fencing.

9

SKY TRACE
Kugahara, Tokyo, Japan
Architect Kiyoshi Sey Takeyama + AMORPHE
Plot size 76m² / 818ft²

1 The outer surfaces are covered in a transparent waterproofing compound, removing the need for gutters or drainpipes, and intensifying the sense of sculptural abstraction.

2 From left: First-floor, second-floor and roof plans. (1) dining room, (2) bathroom, (3) piano room, (4) bedroom, (5) child's room, (6) void over courtyard, (7) roof terrace.

3 Sections. (1) courtyard, (2) gallery, (3) child's room, (4) study, (5) carport, (6) dining room, (7) piano room, (8) roof terrace.

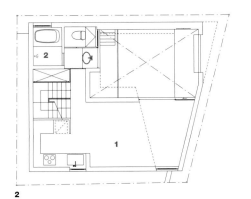
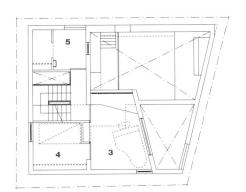
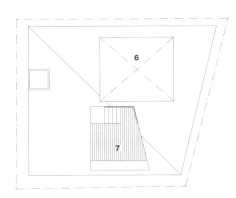

2

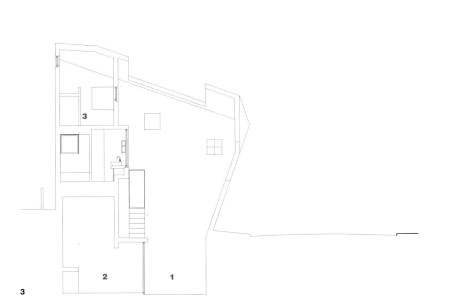

3

Kiyoshi Sey Takeyama's brief was to design a family home for a composer, a photojournalist and their two sons. As well as private areas to stimulate creativity, the clients also requested spaces for family interaction. So far, so normal. Things only became complicated when it was revealed that all of this was to be squeezed onto a cramped, asymmetrical corner plot in the genteel Tokyo suburb of Kugahara.

Planning regulations dictate that the total floor area of domestic dwellings in Kugahara cannot exceed the footprint of the plot. There is also a requirement to minimize coverage to 60 per cent, and to conform to strict height and shading guidelines. It was Takeyama's response to these regulations that explain the building's extraordinary abstract sculptural form.

The exterior walls trace the perimeter of the site, with only one exception, the 'slice' taken out of the road-facing corner, a feature that lends a distinct sculptural quality to the composition. However, pushing the building to the edge of the boundaries of the plot meant that the site coverage restrictions were exceeded. The solution was the insertion of an internal courtyard exposed to the elements that extends the full height of the building, including the two underground levels. As well as circulating fresh air throughout the five storeys, the void encourages natural light into the building's subterranean bowels.

The decision to excavate the site was another creative response to planning regulations. Rooms one metre (three feet) or more below ground level are exempt from calculations about the permitted floor area. The inclusion of the carport was also a means of maximizing the usable floor space: the area of a garage is permitted to exceed standard site coverage restrictions by 20 per cent.

Inside the building, the clients' request for 'a spatial quality to stimulate their creativity' has been achieved by separating the private spaces above and below the first-floor living and dining area. The husband's photography studio is in the basement – generous ceiling heights ensure sufficient depth to satisfy the planners, and obviate any sense of claustrophobia. His wife's music room occupies the top floor and has access to the roof terrace, which is large enough for al fresco family meals.

Every corner of the interior has been utilized. Space-saving features include built-in storage and integrated ladders offering access between levels.

A textured palette of exposed concrete and timber contrasts with the stark white walls of the exterior.

4

4 Local planning regulations minimize site coverage to 60 per cent, which explains the insertion of a full-height courtyard chamber. A roof terrace provides additional access to the elements.

5 The footprint of the building traces the site boundary. The angular 'slice' taken out of the road-facing corner is the only exception to this rule.

6 The courtyard chamber allows natural light and fresh air to circulate throughout the five storeys.

5

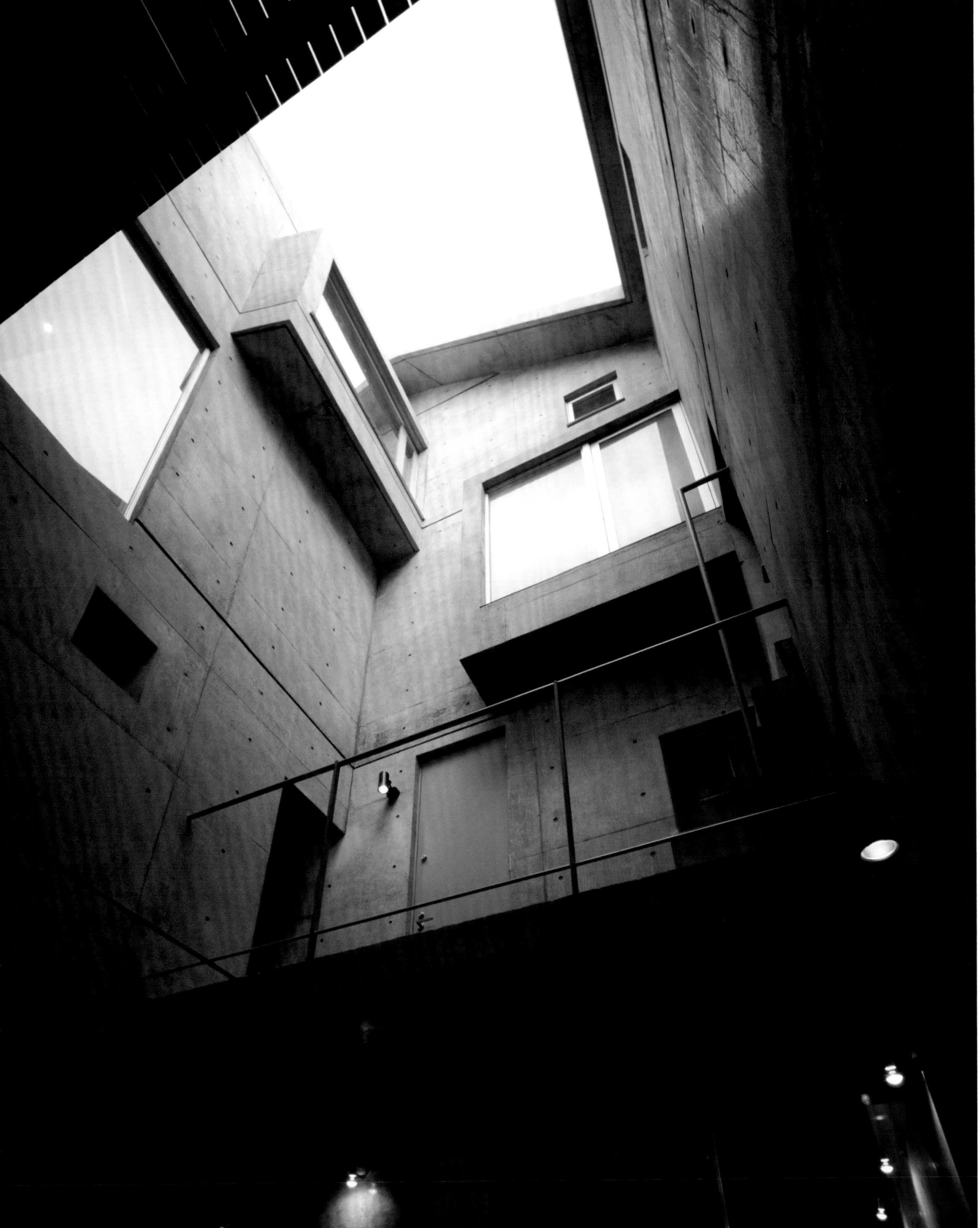

7 Integrated ladders between floors and built-in storage help to maximize the interior space.

8 The mute, angular envelope is punctuated by a series of picture windows that frame views of the sky and streets.

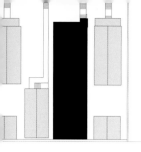

URBAN INFILL 01
Milwaukee, Wisconsin, USA
Architect Johnsen Schmaling Architects
Plot size 279m² / 3003ft²

1 The building is composed of three interlocking components: a timber cube, a long stucco box and an external courtyard formed by a concrete veneer wall.

2 The large picture window on the upper level offers views over the city centre; at night it becomes a lantern on the street.

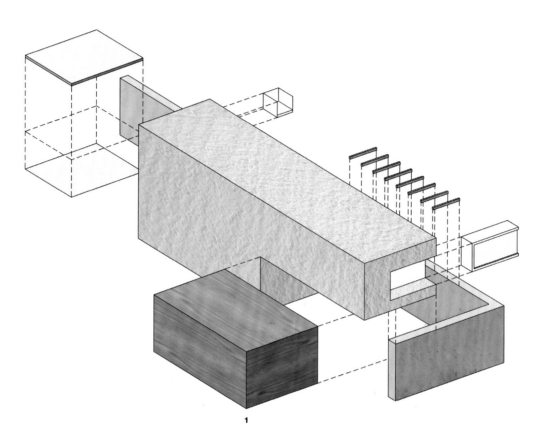

1

It does not necessarily take much to kick-start the revival of a deprived neighbourhood. Studio space for artists or a fashionable bar can be all that is required to begin the process of attracting new people to an area and reversing negative perceptions. Even a small house can have the desired effect.

Urban Infill 01 is a narrow two-storey house on a nine metre (26 foot) wide brownfield site in a district of central Milwaukee that, since the city's economic heyday in the 1950s, has suffered significant population flight and disinvestment. The 279 square metre (3,003 square foot) plot was bought from the city authorities for US$3,000 by a developer who planned to build a rental property on it.

His brief to local architects Brian Johnsen and Sebastien Schmaling was to design a prototypical low-cost production home. The concept had to be adaptable to sites of different dimensions – the developer planned to roll the concept out on a number of blighted sites – and sufficiently flexible to accommodate one or two families. The budget was only US$65 per square metre (three square feet).

Johnsen Schmaling's cost-effective solution was to design a building with three interlocking components: a cedar-clad structure for the entrance and vertical circulation; a stucco box assembled from stud wall panels that can provide up to 180 square metres (1936 square feet) of living space; and a concrete veneer wall punctuated with large openings that forms a semi-private courtyard between the house and the site edge. A sliding door provides access between the two.

Technically, this extension contravenes Milwaukee's zoning codes, which require new houses on infill sites to replicate the footprint of the former building. In theory this should have required a solid mass to fill the plot. Fortunately Greg Patin, Milwaukee's zoning and development co-ordinator, took an enlightened view of Johnsen Schmaling's scheme: 'The architects used the space positively. They came up with a good solution that anchors the house to its lot really well.'

Reviewing the house in 2005, the American Institute of Architects' Design Awards jury was equally impressed: 'It is a small, compact and relatively simple building that was economically built. It has the future written all over it.'

Johnsen Schmaling Architects has subsequently completed Urban Infill 02, also in Milwaukee (see page 11). The three-bedroom house is similarly based on the system of interlocking components, in this case a compact two-storey timber cube and a single-storey concrete block bar. Okume panels enclose the cube. Ribbons of alternating windows and fibre cement louvres with a high-gloss finish wrap around the corner of the cube.

The placement of the windows can be altered within the ribbons to capture views or ensure privacy, depending on need. A set of delicate steel brackets ties the two volumes together and defines the semi-private south-facing terrace – accessible from the upper level – that maximizes the outdoor space on the tight site.

3

4

5

3 Urban Infill 01 is a starkly contemporary two-storey property in a late nineteenth-century Milwaukee neighbourhood suffering the effects of 30 years of economic decline.

4 The semi-private external courtyard, connected to the living space via sliding doors, is a cost-effective means of extending the living space.

5 The second of Johnsen Schmaling's series of low-cost, flexible urban infill houses: a detached three-bedroom property on another tight site in central Milwaukee.

24 RUE DU BUISSON SAINT-LOUIS

Paris, France
Architect Christian Pottgiesser
Plot size 30m² approx / 323ft² approx

2

It has a footprint of barely 30 square metres (323 square feet), yet this miniature split-level house contains a living room, kitchen, bathroom, dining area, integrated storage, and staircase to a second-level bedroom. And remarkably, all of this has been accommodated without compromising the quality of light or sense of space.

The house, which was built as the private quarters for a nanny, occupies the footprint of an old outbuilding in the back garden of a property in the tenth arrondissement in Paris, close to the Gare du Nord and Gare de l'Est. Space is extremely constricted: on three-and-a-half sides the plot is flanked by neighbouring buildings; on the fourth it is overlooked by a five-storey tower. Access is via a communal passage under the main building.

The stepped volume of the reinforced-concrete frame was dictated by the dimensions of the previous structure, and by a quest to draw as much natural light into the interior as possible. A strip of glass is embedded in the roof of the single-storey living area, which rises from a height of 2.65 metres (nine feet) to three metres (ten feet). Another narrow strip of glass, positioned vertically, marks the point where the roof rises from three to four metres (ten to thirteen feet) to create space for the tiny bedroom. These features, as well as the fully glazed courtyard-facing façade, ensure that natural light reaches deep inside the building.

Integrated furniture, fittings and storage space have been chiselled out of the thick layer of masonry that lines the back wall of the long, thin living space. The alcoves include a daybed, a dining table with bench seats and 'shelf stairs' that provide access to the bedroom. It recalls the cabin of a small sailing boat; no corner has been wasted.

An oiled oak floor and Luis Barragán-esque colour scheme add interest and a sense of quality to the interior of this impressively inventive urban infill.

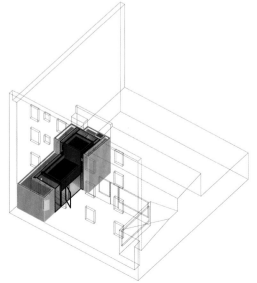

1

1 Axonometric. The house is either overlooked or flanked by neighbouring buildings on all sides.

2 The micro-house under construction.

3 Glazing on the courtyard-facing façade, the roof and at the intersection where the roof height rises to accommodate the bedroom, ensures that natural light permeates throughout the building.

3

4 Like the cabin of a small boat, no corner of the narrow interior has been wasted.

5 Section looking west.

6 Floor plan.

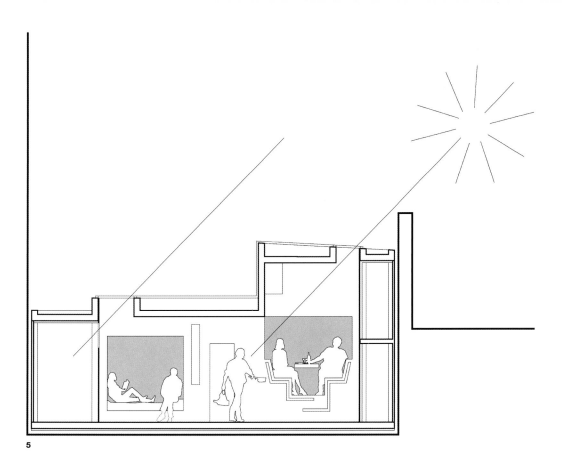

5

6

7

<u>7</u> Space-efficient 'shelf stairs' offer access to the miniature bedroom.

<u>8</u> A dining table, benches and storage space have been chiselled out of the thick layer of masonry that lines the existing brick wall at the back of the living space.

<u>9</u> The dining table, with a small opening leading to the bedroom above.

8

BRICK HOUSE
Milltown, Dublin, Ireland
Architect FKL architects
Site area 440m² / 4,736ft²; building footprint: 189m² / 4,375ft²

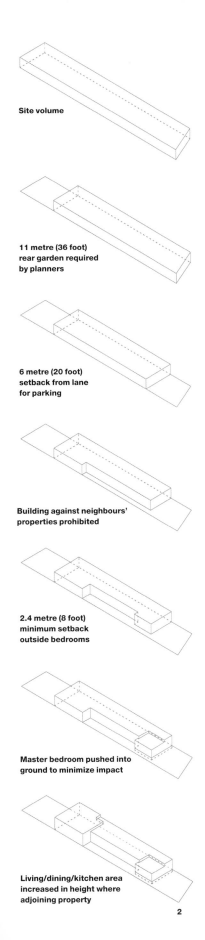

Site volume

11 metre (36 foot)
rear garden required
by planners

6 metre (20 foot)
setback from lane
for parking

Building against neighbours'
properties prohibited

2.4 metre (8 foot)
minimum setback
outside bedrooms

Master bedroom pushed into
ground to minimize impact

Living/dining/kitchen area
increased in height where
adjoining property

2

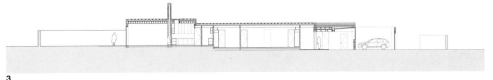

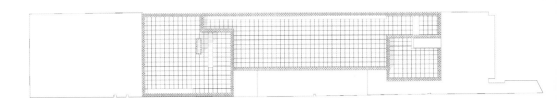

1 Planning guidelines
required 2 metre (7 foot)
setbacks outside bedroom
windows. The space was
used to create a private
courtyard.

2 Diagrams illustrating
how development
restrictions influenced the
shape, form and position of
the house.

3 West–east section.
Vehicular access is to
the east of the site.

4 Roof plan.

3

The Brick House occupies a long, narrow sliver of land left over by the Edwardians who developed this genteel corner of Dublin.

Overlooked on all sides, and lined by the red brick walls of neighbouring gardens, the 53-metre (174-foot) long, 8-metre (27-foot) wide plot was saddled with severe development restrictions. These constraints dictated the shape, form and position of the single-storey property.

FKL architects was obliged to factor in an 11 metre (36 foot) back garden to the west, and a six metre (20 foot) bay for parking at the eastern end of the site. Building against certain neighbouring properties was prohibited, setbacks outside bedrooms had to be at least 2 metres (7 feet) deep to comply with planning requirements, and red brick was the inevitable choice of building material. The designed outcome was a compact three-bedroom house that faces inwards to a series of landscaped courtyards.

The property rises incrementally from east to west:

the master bedroom at the east end was 'pushed' into the ground to minimize its visual impact. At the other end the living and dining area was raised to connect it with the garden and to maximize daylight.

Internal spaces are simple expressions of the external form. A long top-lit corridor forms the spine of the house, from which all rooms are accessed. At opposite ends of this circulation space the open-plan living area and master bedroom bookend the house. An extensive use of glazing and sliding doors set flush with the brickwork floods the interior with natural light and draws the garden into the interior.

To minimize the impact of Brick House when viewed from surrounding properties, the roof became a 'fifth elevation'. Its flush brick parapet blends with the colour-matched paving slab to create a seamless and homogenous appearance entirely in keeping with the discreet and elegantly realized urban infill.

4

5

6

7

5 Rear garden. Extensive use of glazing, and sliding doors and windows, ensures that the house is firmly rooted in the landscape.

6 The bedroom rooflight allows light in and views out to the sky while maintaining privacy.

7 The red brick walls of neighbouring properties define the sides of the long, narrow parcel, and dictated the choice of materials for the new house.

8 Fifth elevation. The roof blends with the topography and local colour palette to minimize the impact of the building on its genteel Edwardian environment.

9 Floor plan.

8

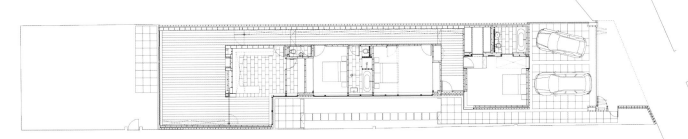

9

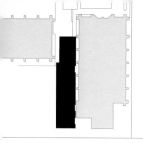

BROOKES STREET HOUSE
Brisbane, Australia
Architect James Russell Architects
Plot size 260m² / 2,799ft²; house area including courtyard: 194m² / 2,088ft²

A contemporary family home and office space fits seamlessly between two heritage-listed nineteenth-century ecclesiastical buildings in the booming Brisbane suburb of Fortitude Valley.

The site of the Brookes Street House was originally a six metre (20 foot) wide car park, sandwiched between a former Methodist churche and its hall near two major arterial roads. For architect James Russell, who now lives in the house and runs his practice from an office on the site, there were several hurdles to overcome.

Russell and his wife bought the church and attached land in 1992 with the intention of converting it into their home. But after living in it for a couple of years they began to think of the site as a 'little village' and looked at ways of developing it further. Russell came up with the idea of building a new structure on the ugly car park and grafting it to the side of the historic church.

He took a collaborative approach with the regulatory authorities, working closely with the Environmental Protection Agency who came to the site every month

for a six-month period to be involved in the design process.

The new building is a concrete, steel and glass box set back 16 metres (52 feet) from Brookes Street so that it is almost invisible from the street. A central forecourt is planted with grasses and unites the heritage-listed buildings on either side. A discreet entry door leads to the new family home upstairs. Tucked below is a ground-level office and car parking area.

The narrow internal staircase opens into a kitchen/living space on the first floor. A central grass courtyard suspended above the car park creates a sanctuary from the street below and sits between two living rooms on the first level. Upstairs, the master bedroom and the children's bedrooms also occupy either side of the open space, linked by a bridge running along the edge, off which are the bathrooms and a laundry.

The space feels incredibly open and light and is suited to the tropical climate of Queensland. Push-out

timber windows regulate shade, sun and rain, and sliding glass and timber doors can close off the veranda space when necessary.

Russell and a couple of his friends built the house themselves, and it is evident from some of the timber joinery that a boatbuilder and fine furniture-makers helped with the interior fit-outs. There are reminders throughout that the house abuts the church, with glimpses of the arched stained-glass windows and red brick walls.

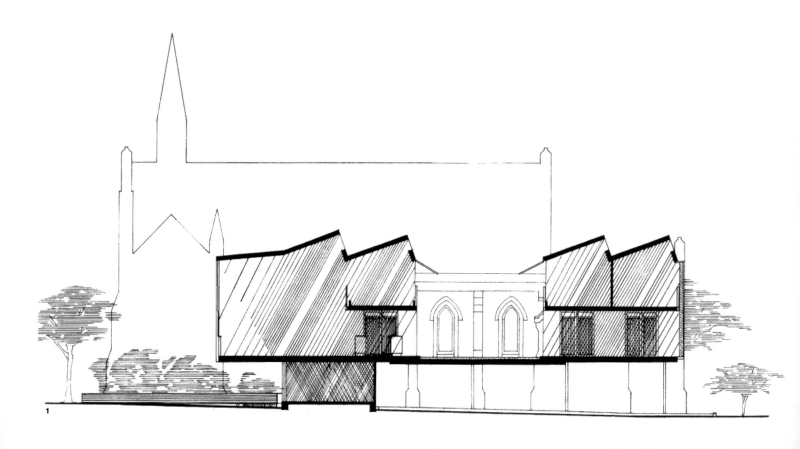

1

1 Long section.

2 What was once a car park between a nineteenth-century church and its hall has become architect James Russell's home.

3

<u>3</u> A central grass courtyard is suspended above the car park and links the two living pavilions.

<u>4</u> The house wraps around three sides of the courtyard with the church wall and stained-glass windows forming the fourth wall.

<u>5</u> From bottom: Ground- and first-floor plans.

4

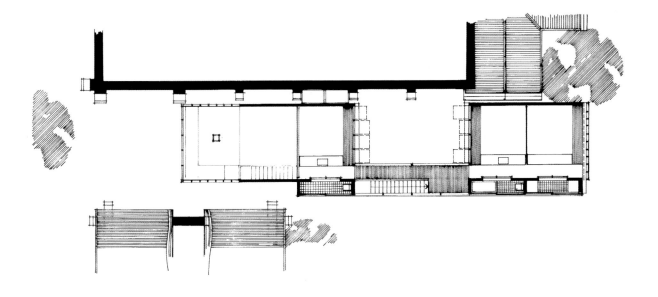

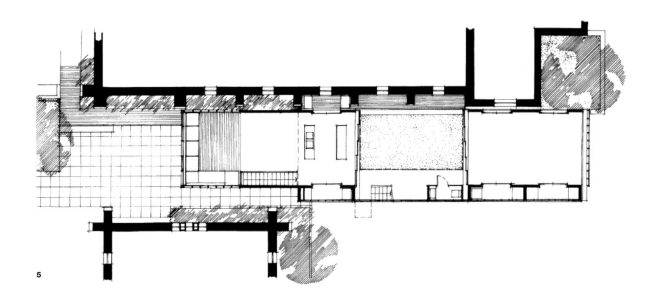

5

6 Living spaces sit on either side of the courtyard – a less formal playroom and a kitchen with more formal lounge.

7 An open staircase leads to a narrow bridge that connects the two bedroom wings and overlooks the courtyard.

8 The bathroom is partly exposed next to the bedroom.

7

8

FAIRVIEW AVENUE RESIDENCE

Seattle, Washington, USA

Architects David Neiman Architects

Plot size 200m² / 2,153ft²; building footprint: 83m² / 8,95ft²

1 The four-storey house has neighbours close on either side but the front façade maximizes views over Lake Union.

2 East–west section.

A significant attribute of this 200 square metre (2,153 square foot) plot in Seattle is the uninterrupted view across Lake Union. It was this waterfront setting that artist and architect Annie Rosen wanted to take full advantage of when she developed the empty lot situated between two neighbouring houses with taller buildings behind.

Rosen approached local architect David Neiman, who specializes in contemporary homes adapted to the Pacific North West climate, to work with her collaboratively on the project. Neiman developed designs for the building's 'shell' – its massing, roofline and exterior façade – while Rosen focused on the details and interiors.

Due to the site's waterfront location, height allowances were more restrictive than in a typical residential area. Neiman and Rosen designed a four-storey building that reached, within an inch, the maximum height limit for the site and filled the allowable lot coverage to the last square metre.

In order to maximize the views, Neiman used a steel 'moment' frame at the front of the house to support a dramatic cantilevered roof and deck on the lower floor. The steel frame supports oversized windows and doors that connect the interior spaces to the exterior deck and provide natural ventilation.

Following the sloping contours of the site, entry to the house is possible from the driveway at the lower level and at the rear on the main level. The lower floor contains a utility room, laundry and guest bedroom, while the main floor is the central living space with kitchen and dining room spilling out onto the deck. The master bedroom and study are located on the upper floor and the loft, set back from the front of the building, is used as Rosen's painting studio. This space is more intimate and contemplative than the lower floors, with glimpses of the water through a ribbon of high windows rather than a full uninterrupted view.

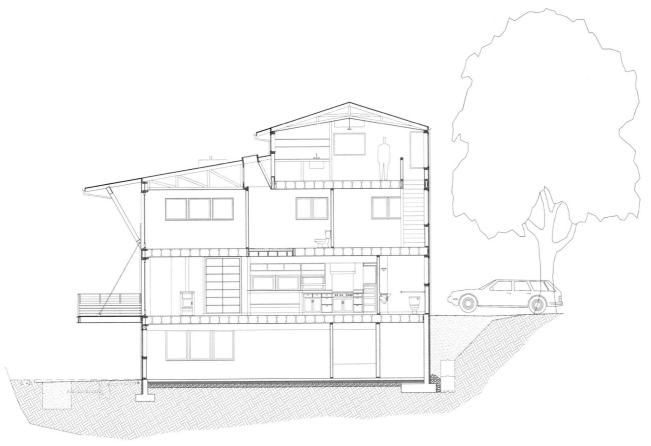

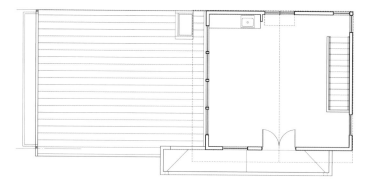

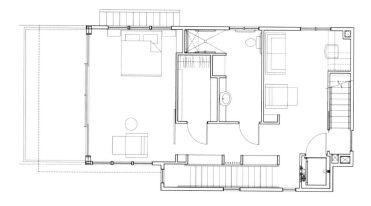

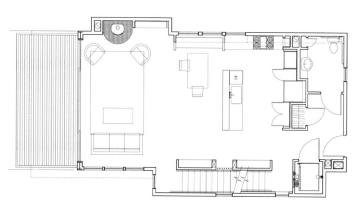

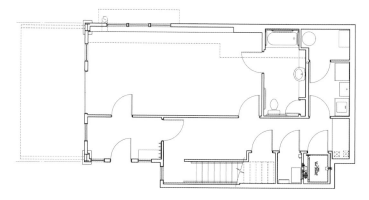

3 From bottom: Plans of the lower ground, ground, first and second (loft) floors.

4 The owner, a Seattle painter, took responsibility for the interior fittings and finishes while architect David Neiman led the design of the building's exterior skin, mass and roofline.

5 Windows in the master bedroom take advantage of the spectacular views; an opaque drape can be drawn for privacy.

4

5

FAMILY HOUSE NEAR LIÈGE
Embourg, Belgium
Architect Atelier d'Architecture Marc Grondal
Building footprint 113m² / 1,216ft²

1 From bottom: Ground- and second-floor plans.

2 The house is positioned on a bend in a side street. Its neighbours include mature trees, garden sheds and housing of varying densities and styles.

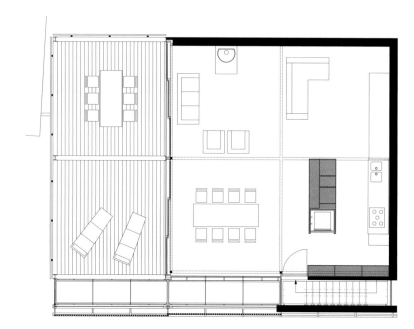

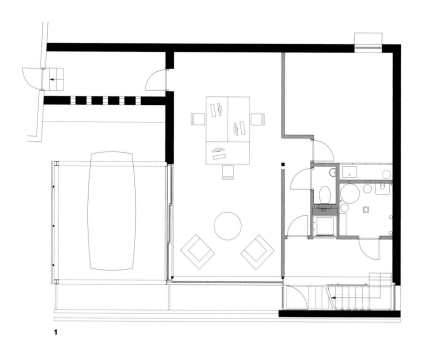

1

Almost every architect of a new house in a congested urban area has grappled with the challenge of integrating the structure into its environment, while simultaneously achieving a degree of privacy for its occupants. In his design for a three-bedroom, three-storey family house close to the centre of Embourg – a suburb of Liège about ten kilometres (six miles) from the city centre – Eric Grondal (partner-in-charge at Atelier d'Architecture Marc Grondal) achieved this delicate balancing act with a particular flourish.

The house is located on a square site, sloping west to east, on a bend in a dog-leg-shaped side street. Its neighbours include vegetable patches, a row of trees and an assortment of suburban houses of various vintages and styles. Grondal's design solution complements this diverse environment without compromising the identity of the new building.

On the street-facing south elevation, a porous wall of timber slats, approximately 3.5 metres (11.5 feet) from

3

4

3 When the shield of timber slats is open the building's steel frame and glass façade are revealed.

4 Timber slats and climbing plants filter views and natural light while simultaneously ensuring that the house makes a positive contribution to its environment.

5 Upper level. The flexible interior can be configured as an exhibition space, apartments or offices, or as an integrated family house.

6 South elevation.

7 East elevation (showing timber shield closed and open).

5

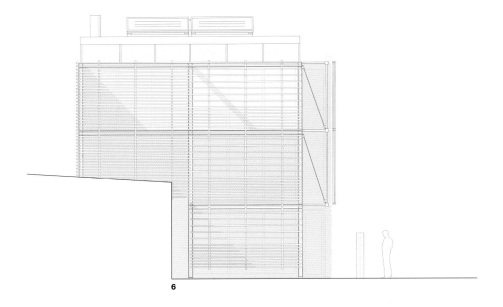

6

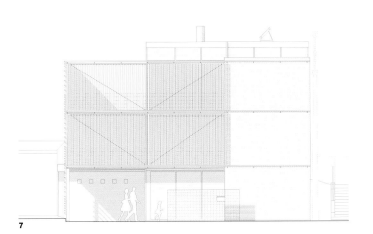

7

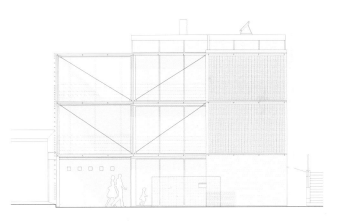

the side of the cubic, flat-roofed house, filters views and sunlight. The slats also act as a frame for climbing plants, which soften the building's external appearance and create a 'hanging garden' effect in the enclosed semi-private external balconies, which are linked by steel staircases.

On the two upper storeys of the east elevation a shield of timber slats, hung from the building's steel frame, can slide open to reveal the steel and glass envelope.

The flexibility of the exterior is matched on the inside. In its current configuration, the building is ideally suited to the needs of a large family. The open-plan living spaces are also used for occasional exhibitions, to showcase the owner's collection of comic books. However, with some alterations to the arrangement of partition walls, they could easily be transformed into three studios, or even an office.

The main structure has a footprint of 113 square metres (1,216 square feet). Concrete slabs and timber decking infill the steel frame to create a rigid diaphragm. The enclosed balconies extend the liveable space from 79 square metres (850 square feet) to 97 square metres (1,044 square feet) on the first floor, and from 79 square metres (850 square feet) to 114 square metres (1,227 square feet) on the second floor.

The low-impact building consumes minimal energy. It incorporates low thermal conduction concrete, solar panels, underfloor heating and a condensation boiler, and is partially heated by a wood-burning fire.

It is also a low-maintenance structure. Materials include concrete, hot rolled steel, galvanized steel, lacquered aluminium and factory-treated timbers.

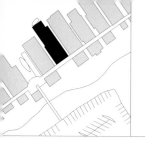

FENNELL RESIDENCE
Portland, Oregon, USA
Architect Robert Harvey Oshatz
Plot size 20m² / 215ft²

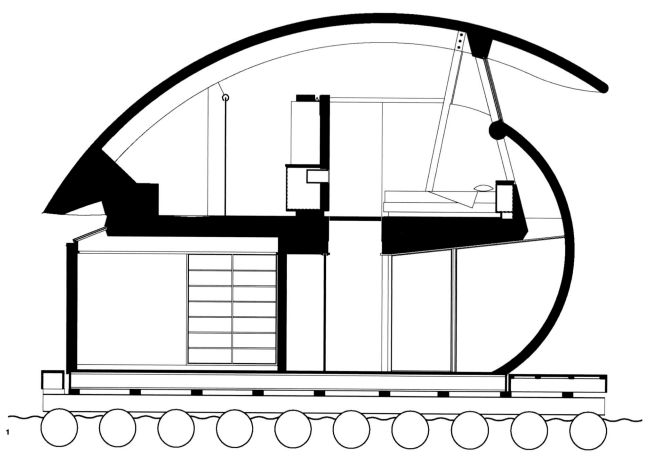

1

The Willamette River in Portland, Oregon, seems an unlikely place to build a new home, but a mooring along the east side is not only a valuable real estate asset but also difficult to get your hands on.

When a local couple secured one of the moorings they approached architect Robert Oshatz to design a suitable structure. The mooring is sandwiched between two pontoons less than three metres (ten feet) away, and Oshatz was required to build a house that could float while providing privacy, despite its close proximity to neighbours.

His clients, who work in downtown Portland, had always dreamed of living on the water rather than beside it, and wanted a loft-style holiday home to use as a weekend and summer retreat. For Oshatz it meant designing a house that was sturdy yet responsive to the movement of the river.

His method involved creating a large float made of Douglas fir logs to act as a stable yet buoyant platform for the house. Steel I-beams were then placed across

the frame and plywood subflooring was laid on top. Cubes of rigid foam were placed under the logs to keep them and the steel beams above the waterline. As more weight was added to the float during construction so were more foam cubes.

One of the most striking aspects of the building is its sculptural, curvilinear form. Finding inspiration in the ripples and contours of the water, Oshatz used Douglas fir glulam beams to form a single curving radius, and cedar shingles were sourced to clad the eastern, northern and southern walls. The western side of the house has floor-to-ceiling glass sliding doors which open to the river, with a curved glass window above.

The 'ground' floor comprises a study, guest bedroom and kitchen, and a living/dining room which opens out to an expansive deck. A stairway leads up to the voluminous master bedroom and bathroom with views across the river. Built-in cabinets and storage areas of Brazilian cherrywood give the space a warm

and cosy atmosphere and minimize the need for lots of furniture.

For Oshatz and his clients there was one final hurdle. They were prohibited by regulations to construct the house on the Willamette River so the structure had to be built on the connected Columbia River and towed by barge to its final mooring on the Willamette. Safely on its mooring, it is a home that is at peace with itself and its surroundings.

1 Section.

2 The Fennell Residence is wedged between two other floating moorings. The west-facing window opens onto a timber deck that looks out over the Willamette River.

3 The contours and ripples of the river were the inspiration for the building's curved timber beam form.

4 From bottom: Ground- and first-floor plans. (1) entrance, (2) living/dining, kitchen, (3) wine cellar, (4) office, (5) bathroom, (6) bedroom, (7) deck, (8) storage, (9) closet, (10) open to below.

5 Street elevation.

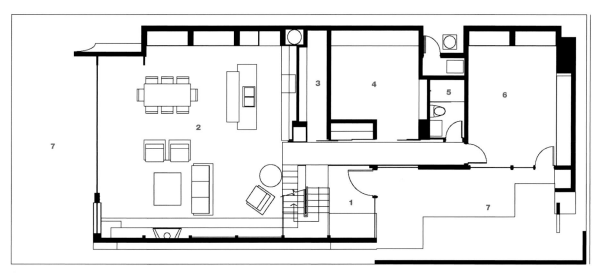

4

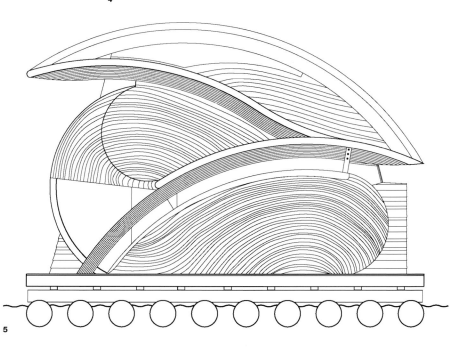

5

6 Internal walls and ceilings are clad in Douglas fir, which creates the feeling of being inside a seashell.

7 Furniture is kept to a minimum, while Brazilian cherrywood floors and stairs contribute to the warm atmosphere of the interior.

8 Glazing on the western elevation frames views across the Willamette River. Access to the timber deck is via an expansive sliding glass door.

7

8

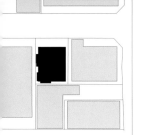

HP HOUSE
Tokyo, Japan
Architect Akira Yoneda / architecton and Masahiro Ikeda / Masahiro Ikeda Co., Ltd
Plot size 50m² / 538ft²

1 Clockwise from bottom: Ground-, first-, second-floor and roof plans. (1) entrance, (2) WC, (3) utility, (4) bath, (5) master bedroom, (6) closet, (7) kitchen, (8) living/dining room, (9) second living room, (10) bedroom, (11) roof balcony.

2 This tiny 61 square metre (656 square foot) timber-frame house has a twisted exterior wall that creates space for an off-street car park.

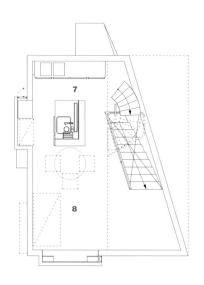

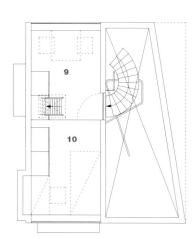

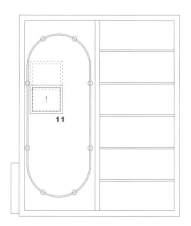

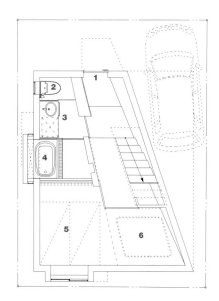

This family home on a tiny site in downtown Tokyo is framed on three sides by neighbouring houses. Finding space for a car park and ensuring that natural light permeated the new structure was a major challenge for architect Akira Yoneda who was commissioned to realize the project.

To get around these problems Yoneda approached his long-time collaborator Masahiro Ikeda, a structural engineer known for finding new ways to make buildings stand up. They came up with the idea of HP, derived from hyperbolic paraboloids, in which the strength of the structural frame comes from mutually supporting convex internal walls and concave external walls.

At the HP House the exterior wall twists towards the street entrance creating space to park a car. Internally, a huge reflecting panel was created to catch the abundant rays of light filtering through the large skylight on the roof.

The white staircase is a central feature of the house with a section of it winding like a centipede from the

first-floor kitchen and living room to the bedroom on the top floor. The internal and external walls of the second-floor space are painted metallic orange and reflect the light and stand in dramatic contrast to the white minimalist interiors below.

At night the sculptural form of the building is reinforced, with the top-floor window reflecting light off the metallic orange walls. The roof balcony is hidden from the street, but provides a calm retreat from the intensity of life in central Tokyo.

Yoneda has made a career out of designing innovative structures on difficult sites. Ambi-Flux, a five-storey pencil building in the heart of Tokyo has an 11.8 metre (39 foot) high void through its core. Like HP, a folded metal stair winds around the light-filled court ascending to bedrooms and a bathroom (see Introduction, page 14).

3 The minimalist first-floor kitchen and living space.

4 Sections.

3

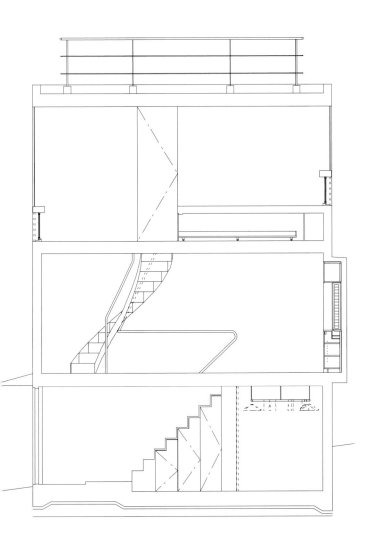

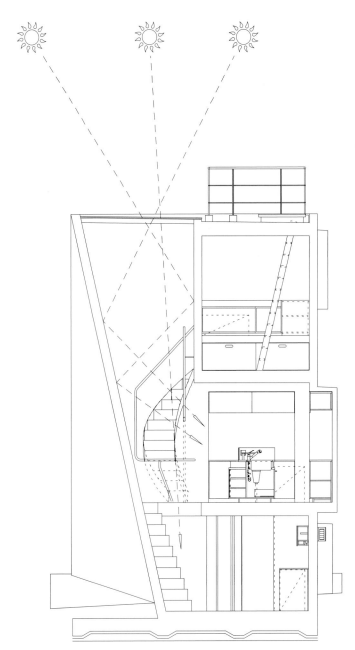

5

6

<u>5</u> The interior and exterior walls of the tube-shaped second-floor bedroom are painted metallic orange in dramatic contrast to the white surfaces below.

<u>6</u> The site is enclosed on three sides by neighbouring houses – a skylight over the roof brings much needed natural light into the building.

<u>7</u> The white staircase is a central feature of the house, winding from the first-floor kitchen to the bedroom and second living area on the floor above.

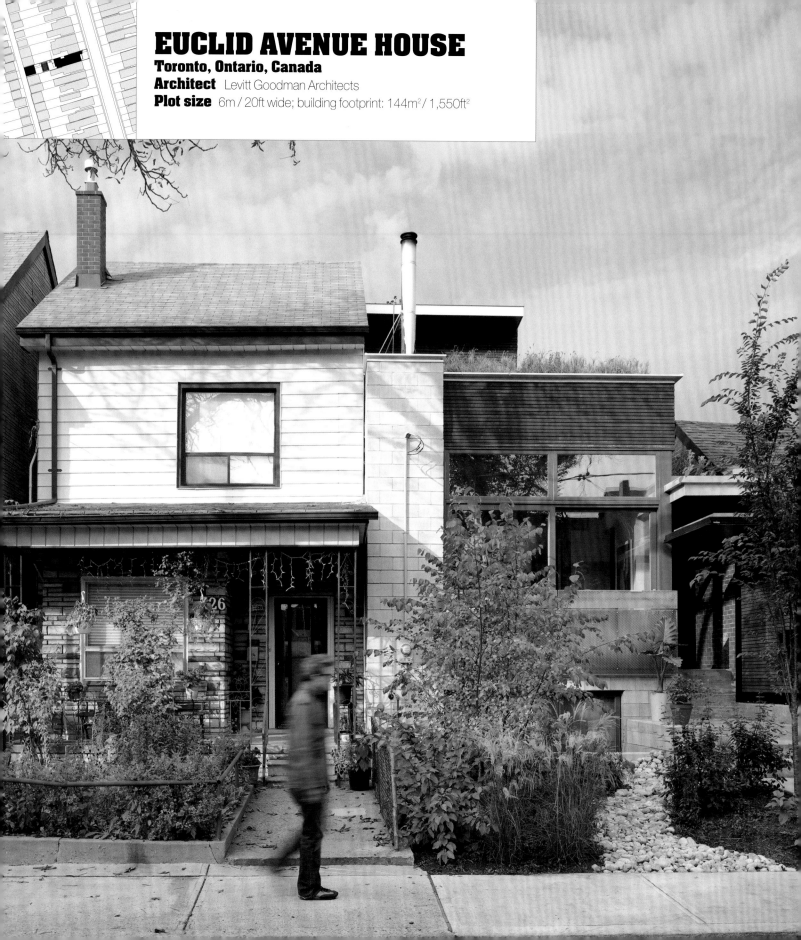

EUCLID AVENUE HOUSE
Toronto, Ontario, Canada
Architect Levitt Goodman Architects
Plot size 6m / 20ft wide; building footprint: 144m² / 1,550ft²

1 Levitt Goodman's 'infill' is set back from the street, sandwiched between neighbouring houses.

2 An unremarkable single-storey cottage formerly occupied the site in this residential neighbourhood of Toronto.

3 A flexible floor plan allows for the basement area to be sectioned off as a separate apartment with access from the front garden.

3

2

This small house in downtown Toronto is a prototype for sustainable urban infill housing, designed to meet the changing needs of one family over several decades.

The architects, Janna Levitt and Dean Goodman, were also the clients for the project. After living in a converted warehouse for several years, the couple bought a six metre (20 foot) wide row house sandwiched between two conventional houses, with the intention of building a new 144 square metre (1,550 square foot) house for their family.

The neighbourhood contains a mix of worker cottages, two- and three-storey Victorian terraces and the occasional house converted into a local shop. The massing and setbacks of the new three-level house were designed to fit within the existing fabric of the street. The resulting building is modest in scale but has a spacious, light interior. The building's exterior consists of dark, stained pine timber boards and concrete block, and blends seamlessly with the surrounding timber and brick homes.

4 Rear elevation seen from the back patio.

5 The green roof is planted with native plants and grasses, and helps to catch rainwater.

6 East–west section. The two-storey house with basement and roof gardens is laid out to suit a family of four but maintains a small footprint on the site.

5

A desire to live in a sustainable manner was a motivating factor behind the architects' vision for the project. Among the most striking features of this house are the two roof gardens planted with a variety of native grasses, flowers and vegetables. An elevated garden space off the couple's bedroom provides a green refuge while the grassy rooftop has a panoramic view of the streetscape.

Large operable windows and ceiling fans moderate the need for air-conditioning in the summer. Natural light floods in from a skylight above the stairwell and floor-to-ceiling windows along the front and back walls. All floors, including the basement, are of exposed concrete and serve as heat sinks for cooling in the summer months and radiant floor heating in the winter.

The master bedroom and bathroom are located upstairs, while bedrooms for the couple's two sons are in the basement which is halfway above grade, allowing light to pour in from the large windows at ground level.

The house was built to suit a family of four but has a flexible floor plan so that over time, when the children move out, the basement area can be sectioned off as a separate apartment with access from the front garden. It is a home that was designed to meet the aspirations of its inhabitants both now and in the future.

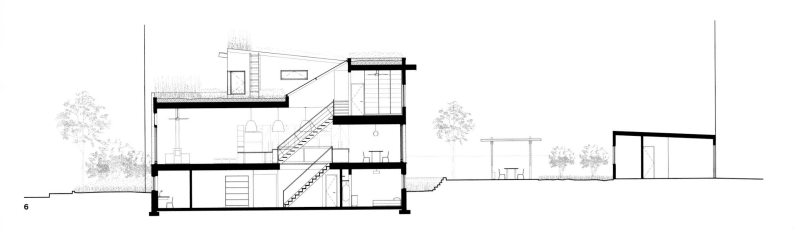

6

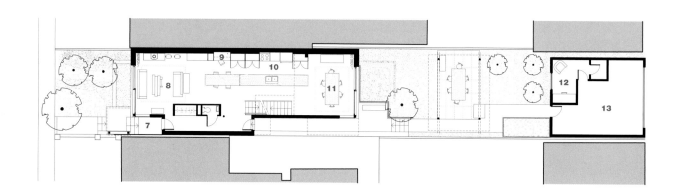

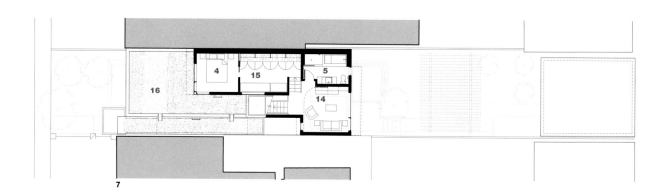

7 From top: Basement (shown to larger scale), ground- and first-floor plans. (1) laundry/ mechanical, (2) TV/living, (3) study, (4) bedroom, (5) bathroom, (6) storage, (7) entrance, (8) living, (9) office, (10) kitchen, (11) dining, (12) recording studio, (13) garage, (14) den/guest bedroom, (15) closet, (16) green roof.

8 A skylight above the stairwell brings natural light into the downstairs living space. Artemide lamps create a dramatic effect over the kitchen bench and dining table.

LOVE HOUSE
Yokohama, Japan
Architect Takeshi Hosaka Architects
Plot size 33m² / 355ft²; building footprint: 24m² / 258ft²

1

1 The Love House is a new building with an ancient spirit derived from Christian values and the story of the Creation.

2 From left: Ground-, first-floor and roof-level plans. The plot is only 3 metres (10 feet) wide and 10 metres (33 feet) long.

3 Section.

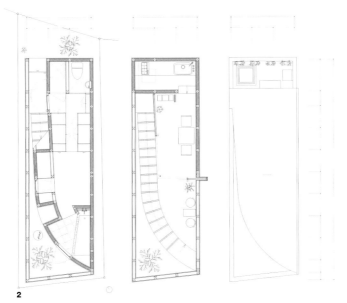

2

Christian values and Old Testament scriptures were the inspiration for this two-storey timber-framed house on a tiny plot in Yokohama.

Architect Takeshi Hosaka developed the concept by interpreting the brief and religious beliefs of his clients – a young couple – through analysis of the introduction to the *Book of Genesis*: 'In the beginning God created the heaven and the earth … [On the first day] God made light and darkness … [On the second day] God made sky and made the ground and the sea … [On the third day] God produced a plant, a fruit tree … [On the fourth day] God made the sun, the moon, a star …' In doing so, Hosaka imbued this house with an ancient spirit.

The centrepiece of the building is a curving staircase that runs almost the full length of the nine metre (30 foot) long footprint. It ascends from the dark entry foyer – there is no artificial lighting in the house – to the first floor at the rear, where natural light floods in through a roughly triangular opening cut into the roof. The biblical reference requires no explanation.

The interiors are Spartan, and the walls painted white, intensifying the ecclesiastical atmosphere. At the bottom of the staircase a door leads into the private quarters, comprising a bathroom and bedroom. The upper level includes two small dining areas, one on an enclosed terrace, the other inside. A kitchen has been squeezed into the three metre (ten foot) width of the house.

There is access to the small rooftop garden, but it requires a certain amount of dexterity: a ladder needs to be propped up on the kitchen surface, followed by a scramble through the roof opening.

Despite its constricted urban location and proportions of the plot – only three metres (ten feet) wide by ten metres (33 feet) deep – the Love House achieves an extraordinary degree of harmony with the natural world. The site is oriented southwest to northeast, so when the sun rises in the east the roof opening is in shadow. By the afternoon and into evening, it is bathed in natural light, warming the interior and providing sustenance to

the plants that occupy the corner courtyard. The roof opening, as well as the decision to embrace candlelight in preference to electrical illumination, allows the atmosphere inside the house to be dictated by the cycle of night and day, and by the changing seasons.

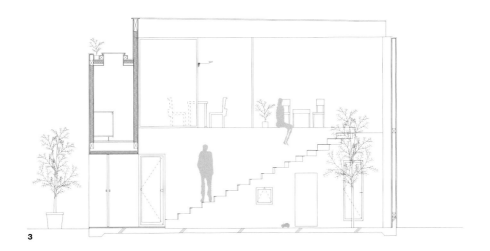

3

4

4 At night the house is illuminated by candlelight, intensifying the ecclesiastical atmosphere.

5 Although a small building in a dense urban area, the Love House is intimately linked with the natural world: the atmosphere is aligned to the position of the sun and moon, and plants occupy the exposed corner courtyard.

6 A staircase open to the elements runs almost the full length of the house, allowing natural light and air to circulate.

7 The site is enclosed on three sides, so few windows were permitted. The cutaway section of the roof and a window over the kitchen are the primary sources of natural light.

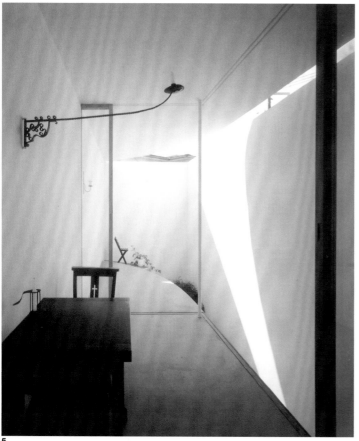

5

6

7

LOWERLINE HOUSE
New Orleans, Louisiana, USA
Architect Byron Mouton / bild Design
Plot size 172m² / 1,850ft²

1 The Lowerline House was built on a vacant site between two traditional cottages in an edgy neighbourhood of New Orleans.

2 Nicknamed the 'domestic shed', the form of the building derives from its industrial neighbourhood and the vernacular 'shotgun' houses, one of the oldest domestic building forms in New Orleans.

3 Section.

4 Front elevation.

143 LOWERLINE HOUSE

Built on the banks of the Mississippi River, the Lowerline House proved its resilience when it remained standing after Hurricane Katrina struck New Orleans in August 2005.

Architect and long-time resident Byron Mouton, and his wife, Julie Charvat, first saw the vacant lot between two traditional cottages on Lowerline Street in 2004. They purchased the site soon afterwards and began planning a building that would be affordable and more importantly, responsive to the climate and to its location near the Mississippi and Lake Pontchartrain.

The form of the building derives from its industrial neighbourhood and is described by Mouton as a 'domestic shed'. The three-storey steel-clad structure is raised almost one metre (three feet) off the ground, rather than being on a slab at ground level, in order to protect the foundations from incoming flood waters.

The house comprises a self-contained studio apartment on the ground floor and a two-level unit above. The second-floor sleeping area opens out onto a deck with views over the Mississippi River. Another deck on the second level looks out over a green baseball field.

Mouton chose materials that were affordable and durable. The exterior is clad in corrugated Galvalume siding on wood framing, steel mesh was used for balcony railings and a chain link fence marks the boundary of the property. Internally the finishes are simple with whitewashed walls and ceilings. The space is kitted out with IKEA furniture.

The house was completed only a week before Hurricane Katrina hit. During the extreme weather conditions a neighbour's roof flew off and dented the side of the new house but, thankfully for Mouton, the rest of the building survived intact.

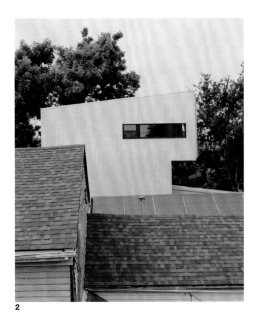

2

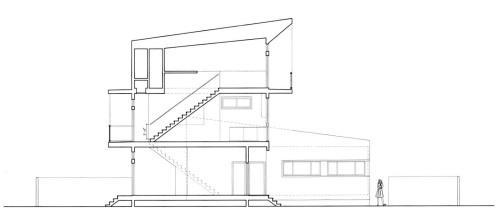

3

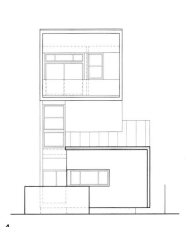

4

5

5 A baseball field opposite the house was transformed into temporary accommodation for people displaced by Hurricane Katrina.

6 Raised almost 1 metre (3 feet) off the ground to counter flood waters, the three-storey steel-clad building looks out over the Mississippi River.

7 A bedroom is screened by curtains in the ground-floor studio space.

8 From bottom: Ground-, first- and second-floor plans. (1) entrance, (2) kitchen, (3) living/dining, (4) bedroom, (5) sleeping area, (6) living area, (7) void over kitchen.

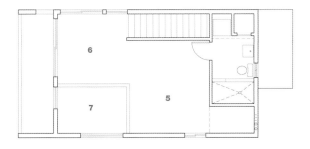

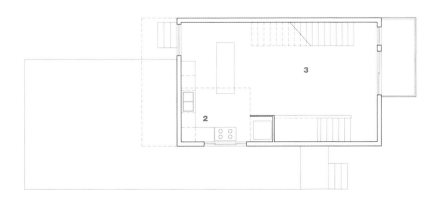

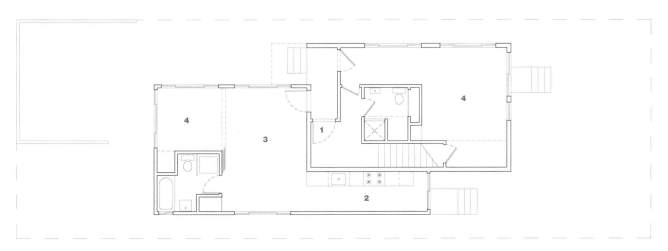

8

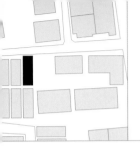

NATURAL WEDGE
Tokyo, Japan
Architect Masaki Endoh + Masahiro Ikeda /
Endoh Design House EDH + mias
Plot size 58m² / 624ft²

1 At night the Natural Wedge glows like a lantern; the envelope is composed of Gore-Tex, polyester and glass.

2 East elevation.

3 Sections looking north and east. (1) garage, (2) entrance, (3) sound studio, (4) living area, (5) dining room, (6) bathroom, (7) bedrooms.

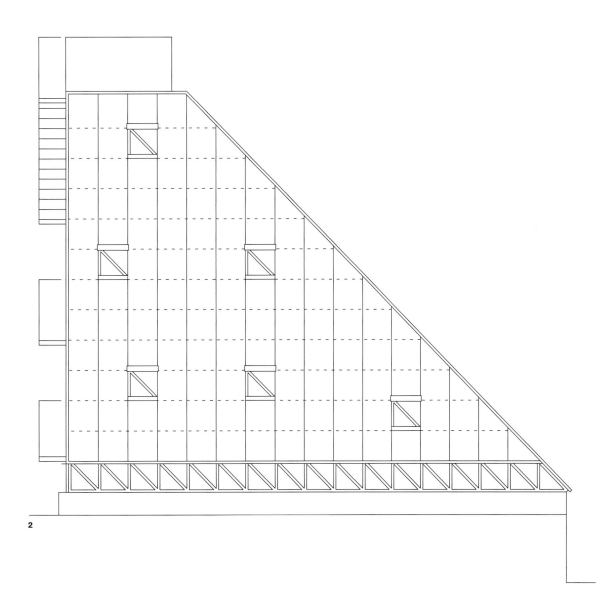

2

Every culture has its own traditions of domestic comfort. Climate, religion, geography and family hierarchy are just some of the factors that may influence those conventions but some aspects of human habitation are universal. Wherever you are, a sense of space, natural light and good ventilation are desirable features of the private home. However, as the cost of urban land rises, and land parcels shrink proportionally, these basic requirements of domestic comfort are becoming ever more difficult to attain.

A young couple with a clear vision of how they wanted to live their lives stretched their budget to buy a tight 58 square metre (624 square foot) plot in Tokyo. Their ambition was for a bright, naturally lit home. They also wanted a building that was distinctly different to anything they had seen before. Masaki Endoh was the architect charged with turning this challenging brief into a reality.

The 45 degree angle of the north-facing glazed façade is certainly novel. It also allows the maximum

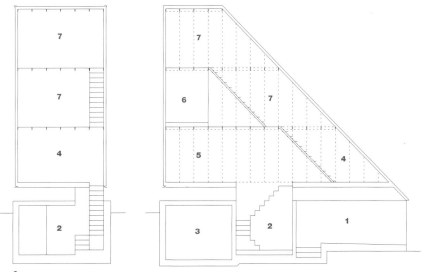

3

4 From left: Ground-, first-, second-and third-floor plans. (1) garage, (2) entrance, (3) closet, (4) sound studio, (5) living, (6) dining, (7) bedroom, (8) bathroom.

5 A garage, sound studio and storage space are accommodated on the ground floor of the narrow plot.

amount of daylight into the space, and complies with local height restrictions. The structure is supported on a latticework steel frame, which spans the narrow width of the site (5 metres / 16 feet), allowing natural light to permeate the clear span interiors.

The materials used in the creation of the building's skin are also very unusual. The steel frame is enclosed in an envelope of glass, Gore-Tex and polyester. Two sheets of glass – which form the exterior and interior of the house – sandwich the polyester, a translucent material with impressive thermal qualities. A membrane of Gore-Tex, another translucent material that also offers UV protection, was placed between the polyester and the external sheet of glass. The effect is a rigid, well-insulated skin capable of filtering the force of the sun. At night, the building glows like a lantern.

The internal arrangement of the house is comparatively conventional. Visitors enter through the ground-level garage, which is also fitted out with storage space and a small sound studio at the rear.

The first floor accommodates an open-plan kitchen, dining and living space; a bedroom and bathroom are on the second floor. The apex of the triangle accommodates a spare bedroom. No corner of this experimental, light-filled house has been wasted.

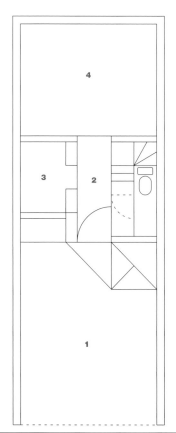

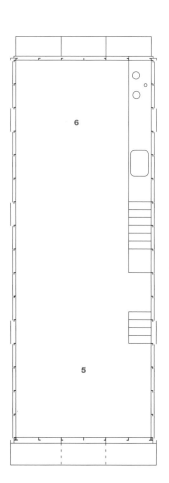

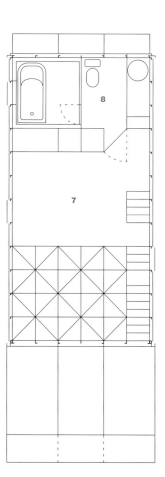

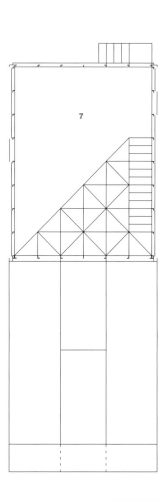

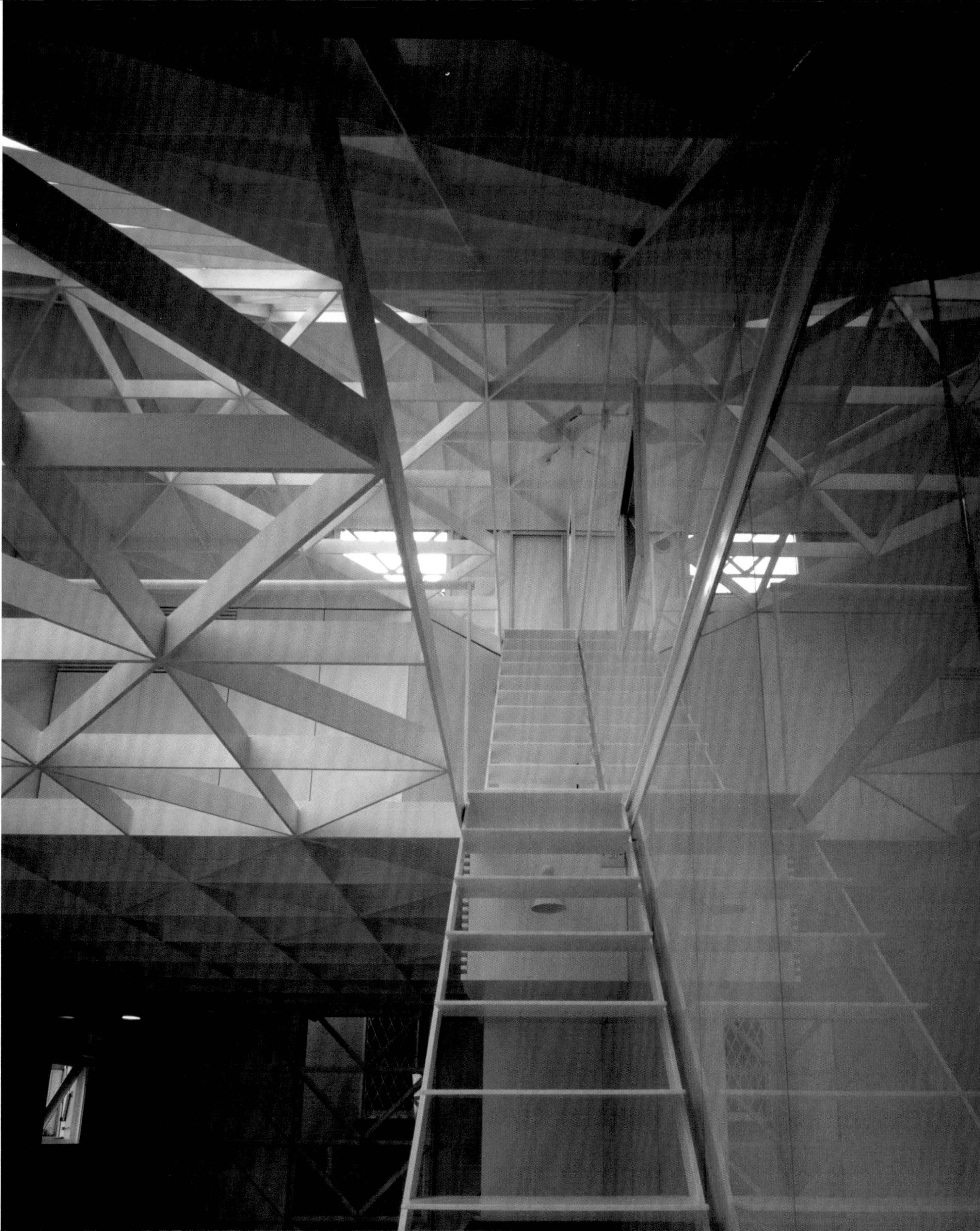

7

6 The clients, a young couple, specified a house with a sense of space and natural light.

7 The latticework steel frame allows natural light to permeate throughout the building.

8 The house occupies a small plot in a dense area of midtown Tokyo.

8

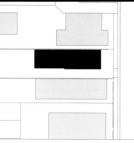

OLD HOUSE
Melbourne, Australia
Architect Jackson Clements Burrows Architects
Plot size 280m² / 3,014ft²; building envelope (including garage): 270m² / 2,906ft²

1 & 2 Jackson Clements Burrows responded to the difficult heritage protection regulations by superimposing a photograph of the original weatherboard cottage onto a glass façade that masks the new two-storey residence behind.

3 The east (street) elevation.

2

A photograph of the weatherboard cottage that previously occupied this site in a quiet residential street near the centre of Melbourne has been superimposed on the façade of its new-build replacement. As one of the local residents has said, 'It is an image of its former self.'

Local practice Jackson Clements Burrows (JCB) believed the former derelict house was of little or no heritage value, a view countered by the council's heritage adviser who took the position that it made a significant contribution to the streetscape. The decision to superimpose a photograph of the former on the front of the latter was a quick-fix and innovative solution to this impasse.

JCB's brief was to replace the original house with a new two-storey family residence. The client was also keen to avoid any time, cost and legal implications that might result from the council's ruling that any new building on the site would need to respond in form, scale and detail to surrounding buildings.

The resulting photograph of the original house, reproduced at 1:1 scale, is wrapped around a series of glazed panels which respond to the predominant hip roofs of the neighbouring houses.

Concealed behind is a new two-storey house that unfolds as a series of protected private spaces that embrace the garden and city views. A substantial lemon-scented gum tree is the only physical remnant of the previous use of the site and the importance of this tree is reinforced throughout the interior with a palette of coloured laminate panels that were sampled from the tones of the bark and leaves.

The house features a wide corridor with a dark stained cedar feature wall concealing a staircase. Beyond the stained wall is an open-plan kitchen and living area with floor-to-ceiling glass doors leading to a deck. A study and powder room sit behind the kitchen.

The first floor has three bedrooms and a bathroom; the main bedroom has an en suite. These rooms are light-filled; most of the windows are two metres (seven feet) above the floor, carefully orchestrated to avoid overlooking neighbouring homes.

The views from the rooftop terrace are impressive, with panoramic views of the city skyline. JCB was able to include a third-level terrace by manipulating the lines of the Colorbond roof so it is not visible from the street.

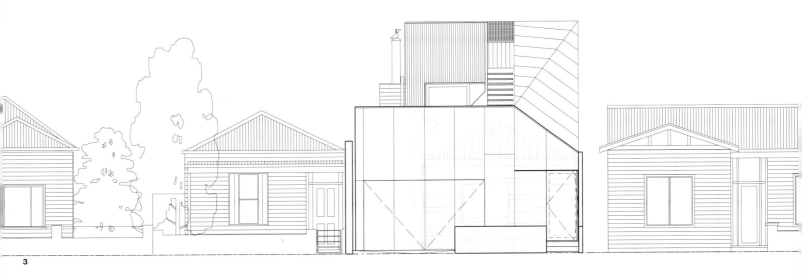

4 The angled roof is clad in Colorbond and the timber roof deck provides views over the garden and of the city skyline but is invisible from the street.

5

5 Floor-to-ceiling glass doors lead out to a timber deck and garden area.

6 From left: Ground-, first-floor and roof plans.

7 Double-limed Vic Ash floorboards line the open-plan kitchen and living space, and multi-coloured laminate panels in the kitchen were sampled from the tones of the lemon-scented gum tree in the garden.

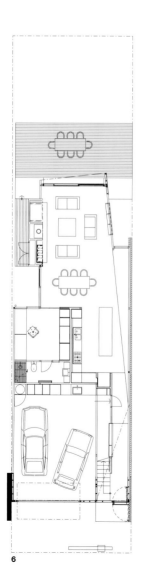

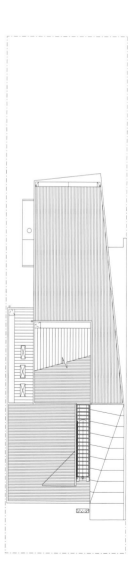

6

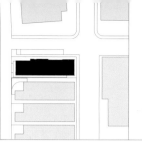

PANEL HOUSE
Venice Beach, California, USA
Architect David Hertz
Plot size 230m² / 2,476ft²

1

Innovative materials and an emphasis on minimizing emissions are two of the defining features of this luxurious house, which is also blessed with enviable views of the Pacific from its location on Venice Beach.

To maximize space on the narrow (9 metre / 30 foot) plot, architect David Hertz used a clear span structural system of wide flange steel columns and beams, diagonal brace frames and concrete decking, so eliminating the need for interior loadbearing walls. An additional consequence of the decision is that prevailing breezes pass unhindered throughout the three-storey house. Vertical air circulation is channelled through the stairwells and the shaft of the pneumatic elevator that links the ground level to the rooftop pool.

Another feature that helps to modulate ventilation, as well as the temperature, is the full-height glass window of the west elevation, which is mounted on a 'worm drive' gear system. When lowered, the living room is open to the elements, and has uninterrupted views of the beach. A system of aluminium louvres was

2 From bottom: Ground-, first-, second- and third-floor (roof) plans. (1) entrance, (2) guest room, (3) beach bathroom, (4) elevator, (5) garage, (6) living room, (7) kitchen, (8) closet, (9) dining room, (10) child's bed and bathroom, (11) media/family room, (12) balcony, (13) master bedroom, (14) master bathroom, (15) gallery hall, (16) bedroom, (17) roof deck, (18) pool, (19) solar chimney/skylight.

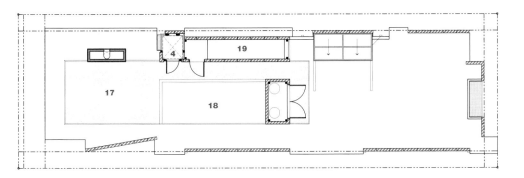

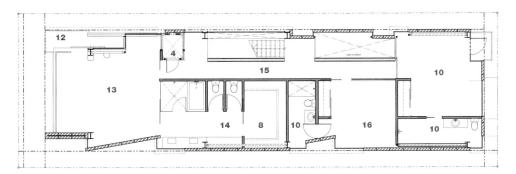

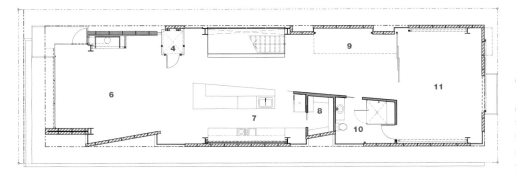

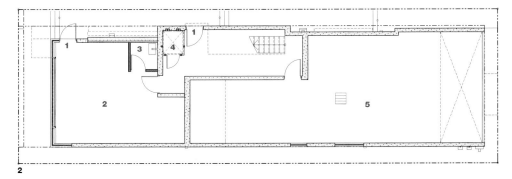

designed to minimize solar gain and provide privacy.

David Hertz, who is no stranger to invention – he once created a house from a Boeing 747-200 – used the prefabricated panels that give this house its name to create a series of angled walls and reveals in the side elevations. They also offer an insulation rating four times greater than standard residential walls.

Typically used for walk-in refrigerators, each panel is nine metres (30 feet) long and 76 centimetres (30 inches) wide with a foam core 15 centimetres (six inches) deep. They are sheathed in a thin skin of aluminium and finished with Kynar paint, an industrial coating that resists weather damage and oxidation.

The use of the panels minimized on-site labour costs, and obviated the need for timber framing. Other environmentally responsible features include: solar and photovoltaic panels on the roof; a networked thermostat with exterior and interior sensors that help to minimize heating and cooling costs; and the collection of rainwater for use in the garden.

3

4

3 Rear elevation.

4 A swimming pool and solar and photovoltaic panels furnish the rooftop, which is accessed from the pneumatic elevator.

5 Ocean views are visible from the open-plan kitchen and dining area.

6 A clear span structural system maximizes the narrow dimensions of the plot, creating interior spaces unhindered by loadbearing walls.

5

LIVE / WORK HOUSE
Groningen, The Netherlands
Architect   de Leeuw + van Zanten with DAAD Architecten
Plot size   175m² / 1,884ft²

1

1 Over ten years in the making, the elevated house stands in dramatic contrast to neighbouring buildings in the historic heart of Groningen, the Netherlands.

2 Street elevation.

A small dilapidated house in the historic centre of Groningen is an unusual foundation from which to build a new three-storey structure on columns, particularly when the basis for the design was a few vague watercolours and a conceptual model of a transparent box filled with green leaves.

But this is exactly what architect Eric de Leeuw proposed to his clients when they were considering how to develop the land and house at the back of their garden. When the couple, both estate agents and property developers, bought the land in 1997 they intended to use it to extend their garden, but this idea was rejected by the local municipality who wanted a built structure to 'front' the street.

The obvious approach would have been to demolish the existing house and start again. However, de Leeuw suggested putting a new building on columns atop the old house in order to preserve the existing sight lines between the garden and the street.

Unusually, the clients and the architect convinced

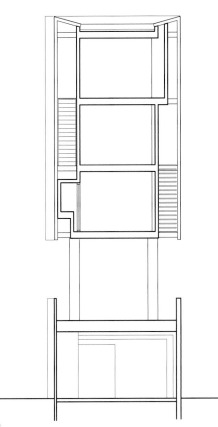

2

3

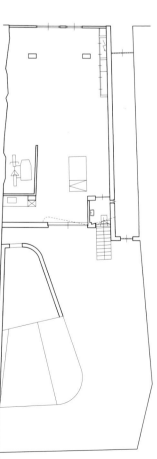

4

3 At the rear of the building a narrow staircase leads from the new structure to the ground floor and garden.

4 From left: Plans of the ground and third floors. The elevated garden structure is at the bottom left of the ground-floor plan, while the top floor contains the bedroom and bathroom.

5 An enclosed glass corridor wraps around the building and offers views across the city.

6 Heavy swing doors in the ground-floor space pivot on a special steel construction and a trapdoor leads to a 'water cellar'.

5

6

the municipality to issue them with a building permit for a 'work in progress' on the basis that building inspectors would drop by regularly to examine the construction. The proximity of the building site to the office of the municipal authority may have been an influencing factor.

What ensued was a design and build process that has lasted ten years. From the outset the clients wanted to build the house themselves so de Leeuw invented a simple 'box within a box' concept – an inner structure containing the living space and an area between the two serving as an enclosed circulation space.

The ground floor consists of a carport (which takes up 60 square metres / 646 square feet of the site) and studio, and the open space between the ground and first floor has an elevated garden at the rear. A kitchen and eating area is located on the first floor and the living space continues up to the second floor. The couple's bedroom and bathroom are on the top level. In the

winter the approximate usable floor space is 80 square metres (861 square feet) while in the summer this can be extended to 160 square metres (1,722 square feet).

The exterior façade consists of glass panels fastened to a steel frame. The enclosed 'veranda' that wraps around the whole building serves as a greenhouse, gallery and stairway. The house is flush with the property on its right and approximately one metre (three feet) away from the house on its left.

VERTICAL HOUSE
Venice, California, USA
Architect Lorcan O'Herlihy Architects
Building footprint 72m² / 775ft² approx

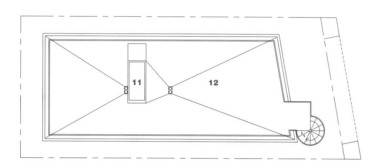
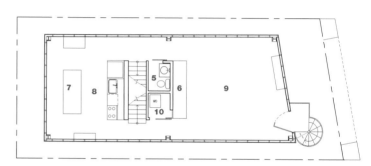
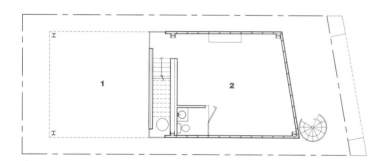
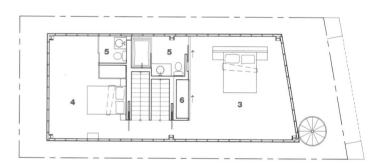

1

Cement boards and three types of glazing were used to create the distinctive rhythmical pattern that defines the envelope of this three-storey house. The outcome is an attention-grabbing contrast to the inconspicuous stucco-clad houses on ether side of it.

A nondescript 1920s bungalow was the previous occupant of the small plot (7.5 metres wide by 15 metres deep / 25 feet wide by 49 feet deep), three blocks from the seafront in Venice. In the late 1990s, architect Lorcan O'Herlihy and his actress wife, Cornelia Hayes O'Herlihy, acquired the by then dilapidated dwelling with the intention of dismantling it and designing the replacement. It was an opportunity for O'Herlihy to experiment. His primary focus was the skin, which he manipulated to give the otherwise simple volume a sense of 'dimensionality'.

A steel moment frame – a frame with fully welded connections to resist horizontal forces – frees the envelope from structural restraints, allowing the skin of blue and yellow tinted glass, black cement boards

(approximately one metre by two metres / three feet by seven feet) and translucent Profilit channel glass to hang from the frame.

The house is entered via a discreet doorway from a path to the southwest of the building. It offers access to a car park to the right and a studio/office at the rear. Two bedrooms and bathrooms are located on the first floor. An open-plan living space, kitchen, laundry room and a bathroom are located on the second floor, to optimize the views of the Pacific Ocean and the quality of the light. The stairwell continues to the roof, which comprises a terrace and a glass-enclosed pavilion for reading and contemplation.

The placement of the stairwell and wet areas in the centre of the building effectively divides each floor into two large rooms, unhindered by internal partitions. As a result, despite the limitations of the site the interior has an impressive sense of space and light.

Another space-saving device was the design of integrated cupboards in the walls of the stairwell on

the two upper levels. The doors of the beautifully crafted cabinets vary in shape, colour and size, mimicking the building's envelope.

2

3 Lorcan O'Herlihy's manipulation of the façade imbues the otherwise simple volume with a sense of 'dimensionality'; the pattern is repeated on all four façades.

4 The roof features a glass-enclosed pavilion for reading and contemplation.

5 On the upper levels storage space has been integrated into the sides of the stairwell. The doors of the cabinets vary in the shape, colour and size, mimicking the building's envelope.

6 The shapes and positions of the windows frame views looking out, protect views in and ensure that the interior is full of natural light.

4

5

6

15½ CONSORT ROAD
London, UK
Concept architect Paxton Locher
Building footprint 145m² / 1,561ft², including the studio and garage

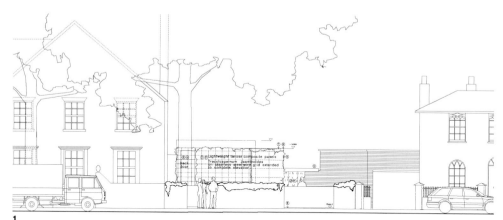

1

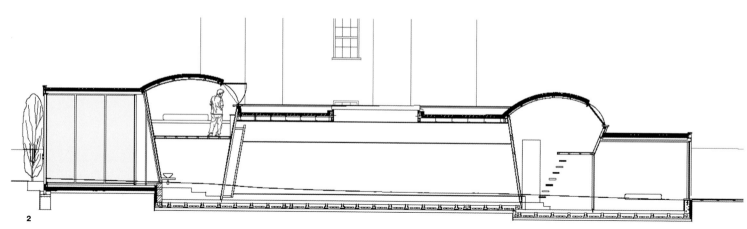

2

Number 15½ Consort Road is full of curiosities, including a bathroom sink in a drawer, a retractable glass roof and a bath under a bed. But perhaps the most extraordinary thing about this single-storey family home with integrated dance studio is the process that its owners went through to get it built.

The story begins in the mid-1990s when Monty Ravenscroft, then an aspiring actor and filmmaker, began looking for a site to develop. His budget was minimal, which would have been problematic anywhere, but particularly in London. Four years and countless disappointments later he bought a thin dog-leg of land wedged between two Georgian villas in a Peckham conservation area.

The site had once formed part of the garden of number 15 Consort Road. At some stage it may also have been home to a garage. At the time of purchase the plot was a rubbish dump populated by two trees which were protected by preservation orders. It took two-and-a-half years to secure planning consent.

Like most aspects of 15½ Consort Road, the process of designing the house was unconventional. Ravenscroft, a keen amateur engineer, was the project leader. He came up with a series of ideas – some realistic, others not so – which he filtered through Richard Paxton (of Paxton Locher), an architect friend who encouraged and steered Ravenscroft's vision. Along the way, there were also significant contributions from MOOARC and FlowerMichelin, both practices an off-spring of Paxton's office.

To minimize costs, Ravenscroft did as much of the construction work as he could. He also called in favours: for example, to avoid the cost of a crane, the steel frame was erected by the muscle power of friends.

It was clear from the outset that permission would only be granted for a single-storey building, and that it could not have any side windows. To overcome the problem of getting natural light into the centre of the house Ravenscroft adapted an idea for a sliding roof

1 The house is squeezed into a narrow gap between two Georgian villas in a south London conservation area. The plot is widest at the front and narrows at the middle, before becoming slightly more bulbous at the rear, forming a garden/terrace.

2 'Mezzanine pods' at either end of the central living space help to stabilize the structure.

3 Plantings soften views of the timber studio/garage from the street.

4 When the retractable roof is open the living space is transformed into an external courtyard.

5 Sloping walls in the living space and bedrooms create an illusion of volume, and accommodate storage space.

6 Ground floor and mezzanine plans. (1) entrance, (2) studio, (3) sauna, (4) kitchen, (5) dining, (6) living, (7) wet area, (8) bedroom, (9) mezzanine sleeping pods.

7 Rear façade. The rear 'mezzanine pod' projects above the roofline. Full-height folding doors and the central roof opening ensure that the house is flooded with natural light.

8 New plantings combine with existing trees to create a verdant 'outdoor room' at the rear.

window that he had been working on with Paxton. The built outcome is a 3.25 metre × 3.25 metre (10.7 foot × 10.7 foot) window over the main living space that opens at the touch of a button and closes automatically when it rains.

From the street the plywood and opaque glass dance studio (or garage) sits discreetly behind a hedge. There are two entrances to the house itself. The main one opens 'invisibly' through the hedge into the studio, and then on into the main space. The withdrawn side door enters a lobby area before the main light-filled living space that forms the heart of the house. It includes space for eating and cooking.

A sense of light and space dominates. Various devices have been used to achieve this effect. To create the impression that the house is larger than it

actually is, as well as to accommodate the yacht-style storage, the walls in the living space and bedroom pods slope. There is also an extensive use of mirrors and glass.

Inventive use of materials is another feature of the house. The walls are composed of lightweight pressed steel, commonly used in industrial buildings, in combination with plasterboard to create a lightweight semi-monocoque frame. The exterior cladding is fire-proofed phenolic plywood, which acts as a rain screen. It is also cheap, and can easily be replaced with an alternative covering, should preferences change.

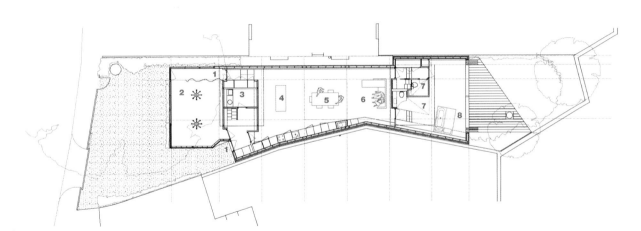

6

7

8

LUCKY DROPS
Tokyo, Japan
Architect Yasuhiro Yamashita (Atelier Tekuto) with
Masahiro Ikeda (Masahiro Ikeda Co., Ltd)
Building footprint 22m² / 237ft²

1 & 3 During the day the building's 30mm (1⅛ in) thick fibreglass skin filters natural light; at night the house acts like a lantern.

2 Lucky Drops occupies a sliver of land at the end of a suburban row of houses in Setagaya, 20 minutes by train from the centre of Tokyo.

4 The front of the two-storey building is 3 metres (10 feet) wide.

2

3

4

Even by Tokyo standards, where land values are among the world's highest, the location and proportions of this translucent three-storey house are unusual. It occupies a long, narrow trapezoidal plot at the end of a suburban row of houses in Setagaya, 20 minutes by train from the city centre. At the street-facing southern end the house is three metres (ten feet) wide, tapering to one metre (three feet) at the rear. Its footprint is only 22 square metres (237 square feet).

The design makes optimum use of the limited site. The width of the house has been maximized by the creative interpretation of a local building ordinance: the requirement of a 0.5-metre (20-inch) setback was circumvented by digging below ground (to a depth of one metre / three feet). Specifying retaining walls of eight millimetre (¼ inch) thick steel plates instead of standard concrete created an additional 0.5 metres (20 inches) of usable space.

The tent-like form of the house has been created by a skeleton of 20 steel arches enclosed by a skin of reinforced fibreglass that is only 30 millimetres (1⅛ inches) thick, including a layer of fibre insulation. The tallest of the pointed arches (six metres / 20 feet), frames the front door.

From the vantage point of the entrance foyer, almost the full length of the light-bathed linear living area is visible, from the kitchen to the bathroom at the far end. The entrance area also offers access to the upper level, which includes a bedroom and a storage area that slopes down to the rear of the building. The metal mesh floor of the upper level acts as a brace stabilizing the steel arches.

The minimal use of glazing is one of the concessions that had to be made to create a house for a thirty-something couple and their cat on such an unpromising plot. The up side is that the milky white fibreglass skin diffuses light to create a soft, gentle, almost ethereal quality inside the building.

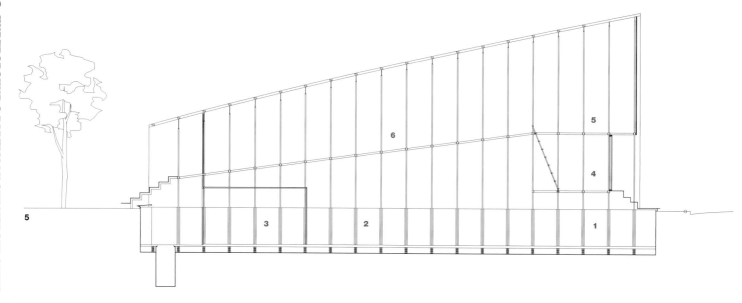

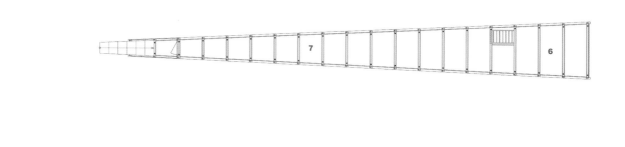

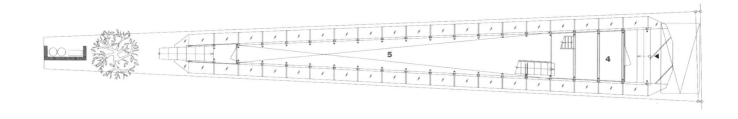

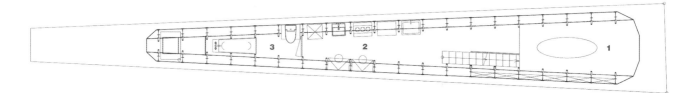

5 Long section. (1) living, (2) kitchen, (3) bathroom, (4) entrance, (5) bedroom, (6) closet.

6 From bottom: Ground-, first- and second-floor plans. (1) living, (2) kitchen, (3) bathroom, (4) entrance, (5) void, (6) room 1, (7) room 2.

7 At the rear, Lucky Drops tapers to a width of only 1 metre (3 feet).

8 The metal mesh floor of the upper level acts as a brace stabilizing the steel arches.

9 The full length of the ground-floor living area is visible from the entrance foyer, which also offers access to the bedroom and storage area on the upper level.

10 The linear interior layout is reminiscent of a submarine.

11 The base of the building was dug 1 metre (3 feet) below ground, circumventing an ordinance requiring a setback of 0.5 metres (20 inches) for above ground buildings.

9

10

11

MICHAELIS HOUSE
London, UK
Architect Michaelis Boyd Associates
Building footprint 208m² / 2,239ft² approximately;
site area: 370m² / 3,983ft²

1 Two-thirds of the building is underground: 1,000 cubic metres (35,315 cubic feet) of soil were removed to ensure that the two-storey house did not exceed a height of 1.8 metres (5 feet 10 inches).

2 Rear façade. The building is a very 'good neighbour', minimizing both its bulk and carbon footprint.

One tactic used by Edwardian town planners to create a sense of space and light in Britain's most built-up urban areas was to leave the occasional plot void. This house, designed by architect Alex Michaelis of Michaelis Boyd Associates in Ladbroke Grove, west London, occupies just such a site.

The two-storey, five-bedroom family home is a shining example of a contemporary residential infill. It generates almost all of its own energy, makes maximum use of environmentally sustainable products and is full of natural light. It is also a good neighbour, minimizing its carbon footprint and physical presence.

Planning restrictions limited the height of the proposed building to 1.8 metres (5 feet 10 inches), the height of the brick wall that defines the front of the site. The idea was to make the house invisible from the street. Michaelis' solution to the problem was to remove 1,000 cubic metres (35,315 cubic feet) of soil and place the house four metres (13 feet) underground. It has been described as a 'stylish

bunker', but this does not mean that it is dark or cramped. The roof of the building, a verdant lawn planted with sedum, strawberries and thyme, is also punctuated by large expanses of glass.

A curved ramp leads down to the front door, which opens into a large white-painted living space unencumbered by partition walls. Natural light floods in from above, and through the full-height sliding glass doors at the far end. A stairwell in the centre allows light to penetrate down to the subterranean level; light wells at either end of the building provide additional sources of natural illumination.

Four bedrooms, three bathrooms, a utility room and a swimming pool enclosed by a glass wall have been incorporated into the lower-ground level. The house also incorporates climbing wall terraces, an internal slide adjacent to the staircase and circular wall openings to create an inside–outside adventure playground for children.

Concrete was the main construction material, a

3

decision that Michaelis reached reluctantly (because of its environmental impact), but inevitably. The options are limited when digging deep on a site enclosed on two sides; few other materials are sufficiently strong to withstand subsidence.

Michaelis made a virtue of the building's underground location by harnessing the natural insulation properties of the clay-based soil to lower heating and air-conditioning requirements – the concrete is impregnated with thermal wool.

Further energy-saving devices include a passive filtered fresh-air supply system with indirect heat exchange that provides fresh warm air to all rooms, and a 110 metre (361 foot) deep borehole that taps into purified water under the earth's surface. A solar-powered pump heats water for cleaning and for the swimming pool, a body of water that helps to regulate the internal temperature of the house. The grass roof retains rainwater and heat. It has also proved popular with neighbours.

During the summer the house generates a surplus of energy, which is returned to the grid. Even during the winter its energy requirements are minimal.

4

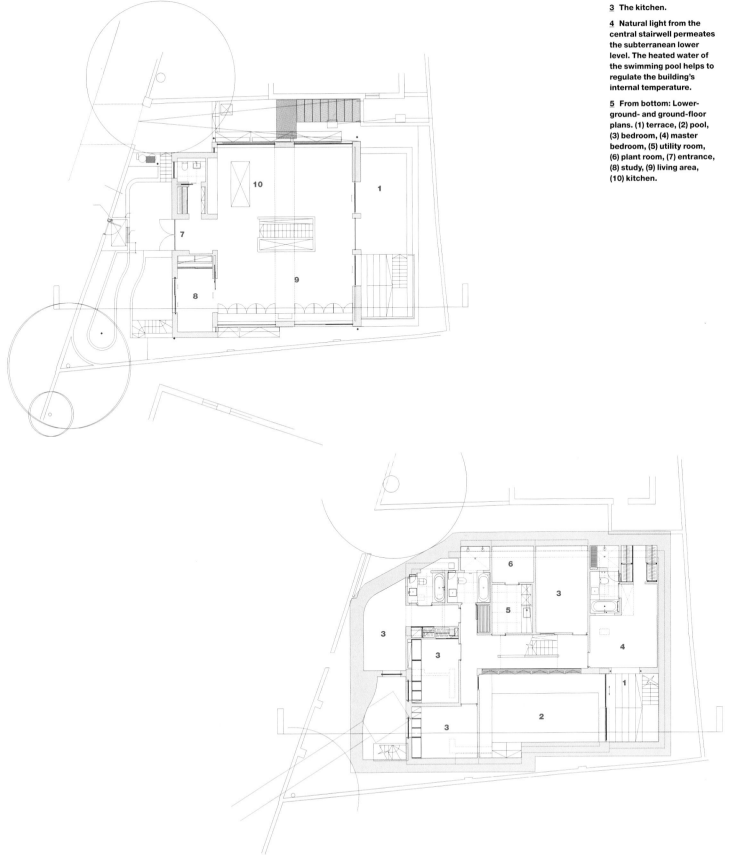

<u>3</u> The kitchen.

<u>4</u> Natural light from the central stairwell permeates the subterranean lower level. The heated water of the swimming pool helps to regulate the building's internal temperature.

<u>5</u> From bottom: Lower-ground- and ground-floor plans. (1) terrace, (2) pool, (3) bedroom, (4) master bedroom, (5) utility room, (6) plant room, (7) entrance, (8) study, (9) living area, (10) kitchen.

6

6 Full-height glass doors
and a large opening in the
roof flood the living area
with natural light.

HOUSE IN MONTMARTRE
Paris, France
Architects Tomoko Anyoji + Yannick Beltrando
Site area 300m² / 3,230ft²; built area: 177m² / 1,905ft²

1

2

3

1 Iroko battens blend with the urban woodland setting; full-height glazing reflects the environment.

2 To minimize the impact of the house on the historic site, its volume has been shared between two components: the main house, to the south, and a guest wing/office in the northeast.

3 Trees, lamp posts, a drinking fountain and the garden itself are remnants of the *guinguette* that occupied the site during the nineteenth century.

4 Section through the house and site.

5 The site, which is surrounded by trees and has been largely untouched since the late nineteenth century, is a forgotten corner of Montmartre village.

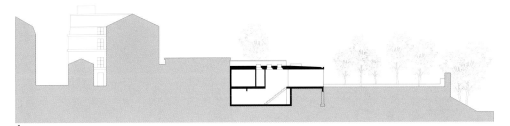

4

Nobody is sure when *guinguettes* first emerged. The origins of the word are also open to debate with sour wine being one possibility. But what is certain is that these informal outdoor cabarets/restaurants, which flourished from the mid-eighteenth to the late nineteenth centuries, occupy a special place in French hearts, particularly in and around the capital.

On Sundays, festivals and feast days, Parisians would gather to eat and drink, followed by a slow waltz to the sound of an accordion. The louche goings-on were recorded by, among others, Emile Zola, Guy de Maupassant, Vincent van Gogh and Auguste Renoir, whose *Le Déjeuner des Canotiers* was set in the *guinguette* at Maison Fournaise, Chatou.

Today few of these spaces remain, but they are fondly remembered. It was out of respect for this nostalgia that architects Tomoko Anyoji and Yannick Beltrando approached the design of this private house, which occupies the site of a once famous *guinguette* in the heart of Montmartre village.

As well as retaining all the surviving nineteenth-century features, including a drinking fountain, iron street lamps and the walls of neighbouring properties, Anyoji and Beltrando sought to minimize the impact of the new house by dividing its volume into two separate dwellings: the main L-shaped house hugging a wall to the south, and a smaller property, with a guest room and office, in the northeast corner.

The foundations of both buildings were sunk into the ground, to ensure that their rooflines did not extend beyond the height of the boundary walls. The southeast of the main house, above the entrance, was dug out to create space for a below-grade living area and shower room.

The layout of the interior mirrors the open and accessible approach taken to the arrangement of the buildings. Partition walls have been kept to a minimum; seminato flooring unites the internal spaces.

The form of the houses and the techniques used in their construction were influenced by the comparative

5

6 Access is via a network of courtyards and passages. The street entrance, on rue Saint-Rustique, is 50 metres (164 feet) away.

7 The inaccessibility of the site dictated the selection of a metal-framed structure over reinforced concrete.

8 From bottom: Basement and ground-floor plans. (1) plant room, (2) shower room, (3) TV room, (4) main bedroom, (5) WC, (6) entrance, (7) kitchen/dining/living, (8) office, (9) bathroom, (10) guest room, (11) storage.

9 Natural light floods the open-plan living and cooking space in the main house.

inaccessibility of the site. Despite its location in the 18th arrondissement, a stone's throw from the tourist masses, it is almost completely hidden from view. Access is via a series of courtyards and passages; the street entrance is 50 metres (164 feet) away. This meant that every component used in the construction of the houses, and the tools used to make them stand up, had to be carried by muscle power. It was principally for this reason that a metal-framed structure was chosen over reinforced concrete.

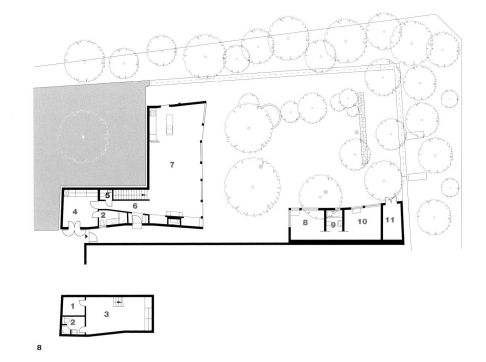

8

9

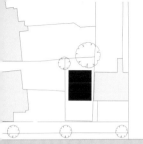

SUNKEN HOUSE
London, UK
Architect Adjaye Associates
Plot size 148m²/1,600 ft²; floor area: 185m² / 2,000ft²

1 A wooden cube recently completed by Adjaye Associates ends a row of solid brick houses in northeast London.

2 North–south section. The site was excavated to basement level creating a sunken concrete slab on which the house is placed.

3 West elevation. A large picture window in the top-floor living room provides views over neighbouring gardens and trees.

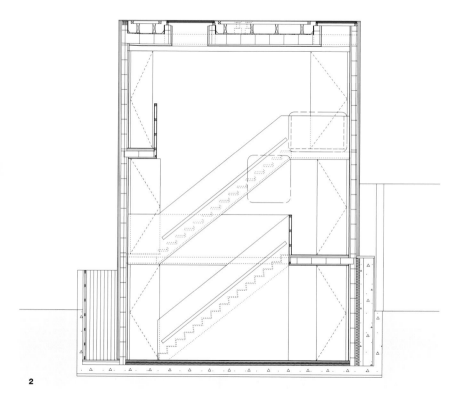

2

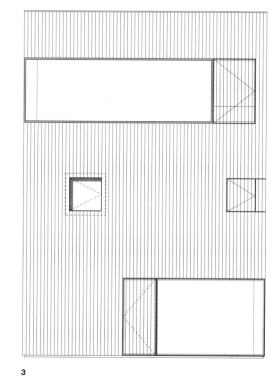

3

The timber building at the end of a row of Victorian semi-detached houses in De Beauvoir Town, northeast London, is a striking anomaly. Surrounded as it is by solid brick houses with slate pitched roofs and chimney stacks, the wooden cube stands out as a statement of discreet modernism.

The empty site was purchased by London-based photographer Ed Reeve who appointed architect and close friend David Adjaye to design a three-storey house that maximized views over the neighbouring gardens to the west.

The entire site was excavated to basement level creating a sunken concrete slab on which the house was placed. Adjaye designed a solid timber super-structure that would improve the thermal and acoustic performance of the building and reduce its carbon footprint. The prefabricated timber panels were trucked onto the site and assembled over two days by a company that specializes in engineered timber systems that can be quickly erected. The timber used

to clad the exterior has been stained a rich, dark brown and hemp was used to insulate the walls.

Entry to the house is at street level via a path that sits above the lower-ground-floor roof. The kitchen and dining room are located in the excavated basement and connect to the garden. Bedrooms occupy the ground floor. The master bedroom has an impressive south-facing window made of translucent white glass against which the bamboo in a neighbour's garden creates dramatic shadows. A living space on the top floor has a long picture window along the west wall looking out over rows of neighbouring gardens.

The front of the house faces east towards the industrial buildings opposite. Timber and glass openings punctuate the building. Remarkably, it only took eight weeks for the local planning authority to issue a permit for the design. The application also had to go before the conservation committee. According to Reeve the committee were happy with the plans as long as the new structure followed the existing building

line along the street, and the eaves line of the neighbouring houses.

In an area where there is a lot of subsidence the concrete foundation is likely to ensure that the building will be standing long after the Victorian structures around it.

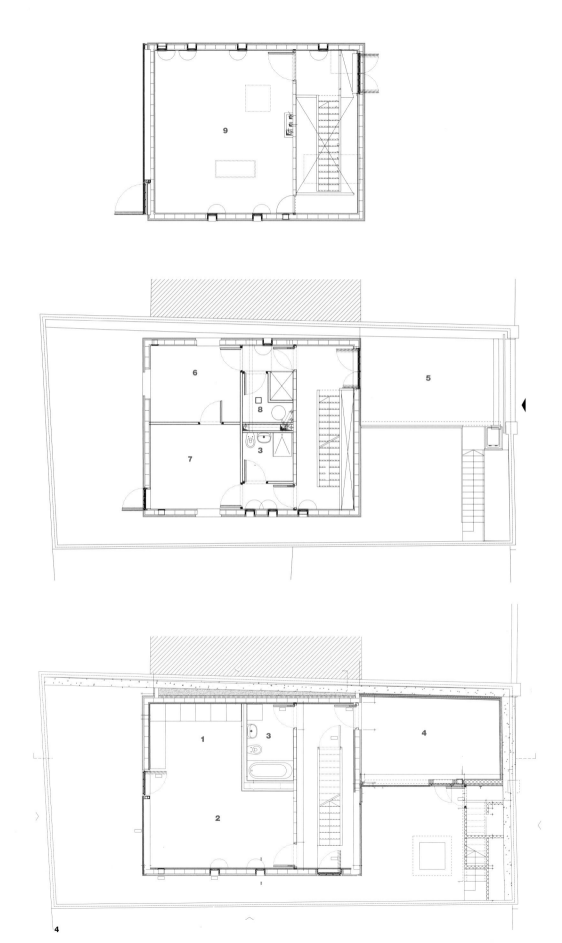

4

4 From bottom: Basement, ground- and first-floor plans. (1) kitchen, (2) dining room, (3) bathroom, (4) study, (5) deck terrace, (6) nursery, (7) bedroom, (8) utility room, (9) living room.

5 A crafted timber staircase is framed by a window and light well in the triple-height ceiling.

6 Dappled light permeates the top-floor living room space.

5

6

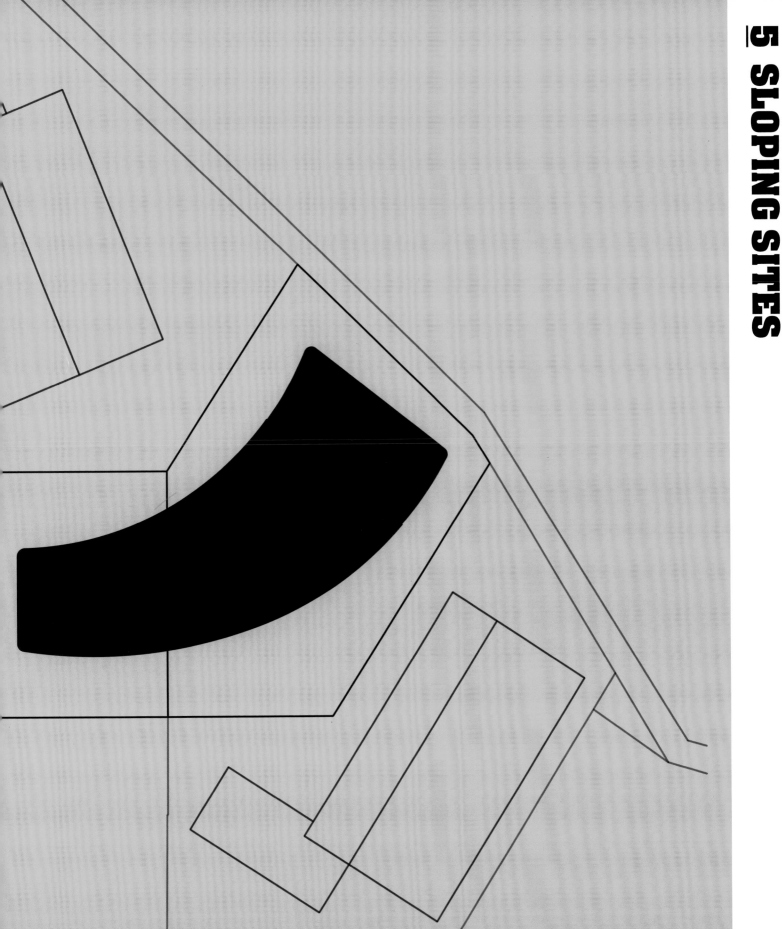

HILL HOUSE
Pacific Palisades, California, USA
Architect Johnston Marklee & Associates
Plot size 125m² / 1,345ft²

1 In some places the small, asymmetrical site slopes at 47 degrees.

2 Section looking south.

3 Tapering the top and bottom of the house helps to minimize its bulk and prominence on the side of Santa Monica Canyon.

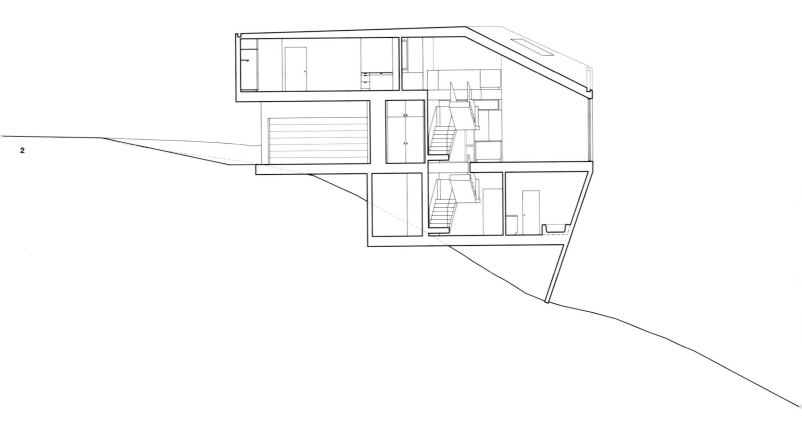

2

3

Designing a spacious house for a small, asymmetrical plot on a steep slope would be challenging anywhere. But when the site is in a neighbourhood with impressive architectural pedigree – the Eames House is nearby – and overlooks protected views of Santa Monica Canyon, the scale of the task becomes monumental. This was the conundrum facing architects Sharon Johnston and Mark Lee.

The angular, cut diamond form of the building's envelope is explained by the architects' strategy for complying with local seismic codes, coastal regulations and hillside ordinances on bulk and height (15 metres / 49 feet from the lowest point). Essentially, they sought to maximize the volume of the house while minimizing its footprint.

Tapering the top and bottom of the canyon-facing side was a significant part of this strategy, but not to the detriment of the spatial qualities of the interior, of which the highlight is the double-height living and dining area, which takes up the bulk of the ground floor. The room

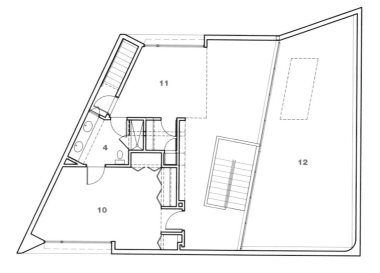

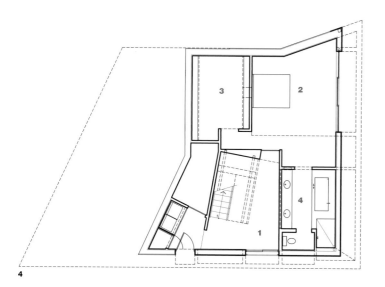

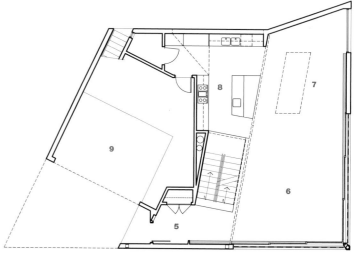

4

has an epic sense of scale and light, thanks to the insertion of a mezzanine level and the extensive use of glass, offering expansive views over the canyon to the south and east.

As well as the communal areas and the kitchen, the ground floor contains the entrance and garage. The private areas are positioned above and below: the master bedroom, a sunroom and bathroom are on the lower ground floor; the mezzanine contains a study, bathroom and spare bedroom.

The foundation of the house, based on nine 12 metre (39 foot) deep reinforced-concrete piles, is anchored in the bedrock. A braced steel frame with timber infill framing emerges out of the concrete base to form the circulation core and cantilevered overhang at the entry.

The building is finished in an elastic and cement composite skin, which creates a seamless seal around the angular structure. The embedded lavender colour of the coating was taken from the pigment of

eucalyptus bark, prevalent at the site, reinforcing the building's connections with the landscape.

Eighteen months after design work on the Hill House began, Johnston Marklee's client withdrew from the project. But rather than giving up, the architects – a young couple who met at Herzog & de Meuron's studio at the Harvard Graduate School of Design – raised the funds to continue. Two years later, when the house was complete, it sold quickly. The buyer was a designer noted for her cutting-edge jewellery and clothes. It was a perfect fit.

5

6

4 Anti-clockwise from bottom left: Lower ground-, ground- and mezzanine plans. (1) sun room, (2) master bedroom, (3) closet, (4) bathroom, (5) entrance, (6) living room, (7) dining room, (8) kitchen, (9) garage, (10) bedroom, (11) study, (12) void.

5 A guest bedroom cantilevers out over the ground-level entrance.

6 The deep windows frame views looking out, and limit views in.

<u>7</u> A central staircase offers access between the three levels of the hillside house.

<u>8</u> View from the mezzanine above the ground-level kitchen and dining area.

<u>9</u> The open-plan living and dining area has an epic spatial quality, with expansive views over the canyon.

8

9

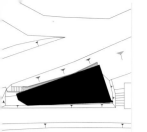

ROOFTECTURE S
Kobe, Japan
Architect Shuhei Endo Architect Institute
Plot size 50m² / 538ft² approx

<u>1</u> The two-storey house is perched on a tapering triangle of land adjacent to a granite and concrete retaining wall.

<u>2</u> Section looking north.

<u>3</u> Section looking west.

<u>4</u> Sea views are unobstructed from the lower level courtyard and *doma*.

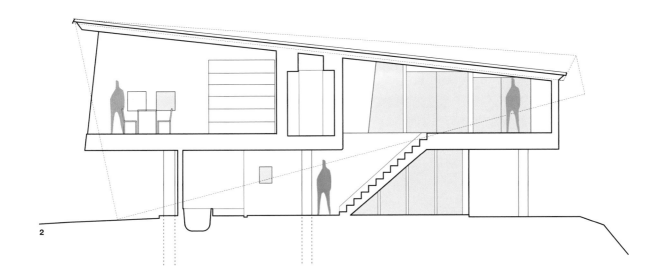

2

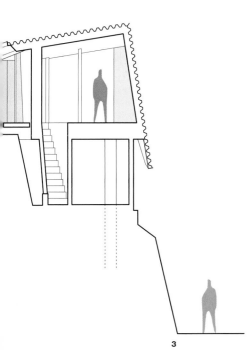

3

The site of this small, steel-sheathed house in a well-established residential district of Kobe made up only 20 per cent of the total cost. It seems that past generations had dismissed the slim, tapering triangular plot on a cliff overlooking Setonaikai (Inland Sea) as unfit for development. But that did not bother the enterprising couple who bought it, and it certainly did not faze architect Shuhei Endo, a young architect from nearby Osaka with a reputation for designing innovative free-form buildings, many of them enclosed in sheets of corrugated steel.

The site – 20 metres (66 feet) long, four metres (13 feet) wide to the east, tapering to 1.5 metres (five feet) on the western edge – is wedged against a north-facing granite and concrete retaining wall, so Endo did not have a great deal of room to manoeuvre, but he still managed to create a spacious two-storey house with outdoor space, enclosed within a shield of his trademark metal.

Five piles carry the load of the house to a strip of level ground below. The gap between the house and the wall is spanned by a cantilevered terrace, which leads visitors onto the upper level. The thin end of the wedge, enclosing a gallery kitchen and dining area, is on the right. A living room and bedroom are accommodated at the broader end of the triangle. A staircase leads from the living space on the upper level to the *doma* – a traditional Japanese room, part domestic work area and part entrance – below which there is access to the sheltered courtyard.

Endo's decision to enclose the house in an angular envelope of galvanized steel has implications both internally and externally. On the inside, sea views from the upper level are controlled; from the *doma* below they are uninterrupted. Externally, the triangular form recalls a shield; a line of defence for the exposed and apparently precarious structure.

4

5 The angular steel shield encloses the volume, framing views on the upper level and protecting the building from sea winds.

6 A short flight of steps leads from the road to a cantilevered entrance terrace.

<u>7</u> A galley kitchen and dining area occupy the narrow end of the triangular footprint.

<u>8</u> The broader end of the upper level includes the main living space and bedroom. A staircase offers access to the *doma*, courtyard, bathroom and toilet below.

<u>9</u> From bottom: Lower- and upper-level plans. (1) kitchen/dining, (2) entrance, (3) WC, (4) living room, (5) bedroom, (6) terrace, (7) bathroom, (8) *doma*, (9) courtyard

7

8

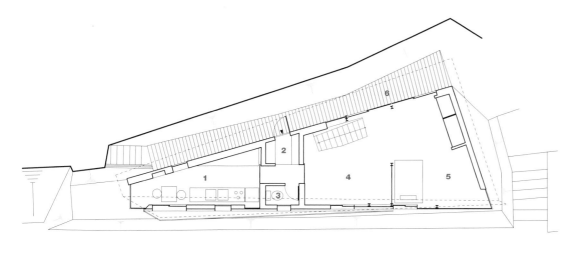

9

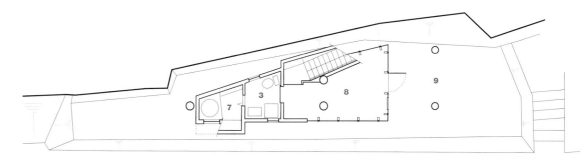

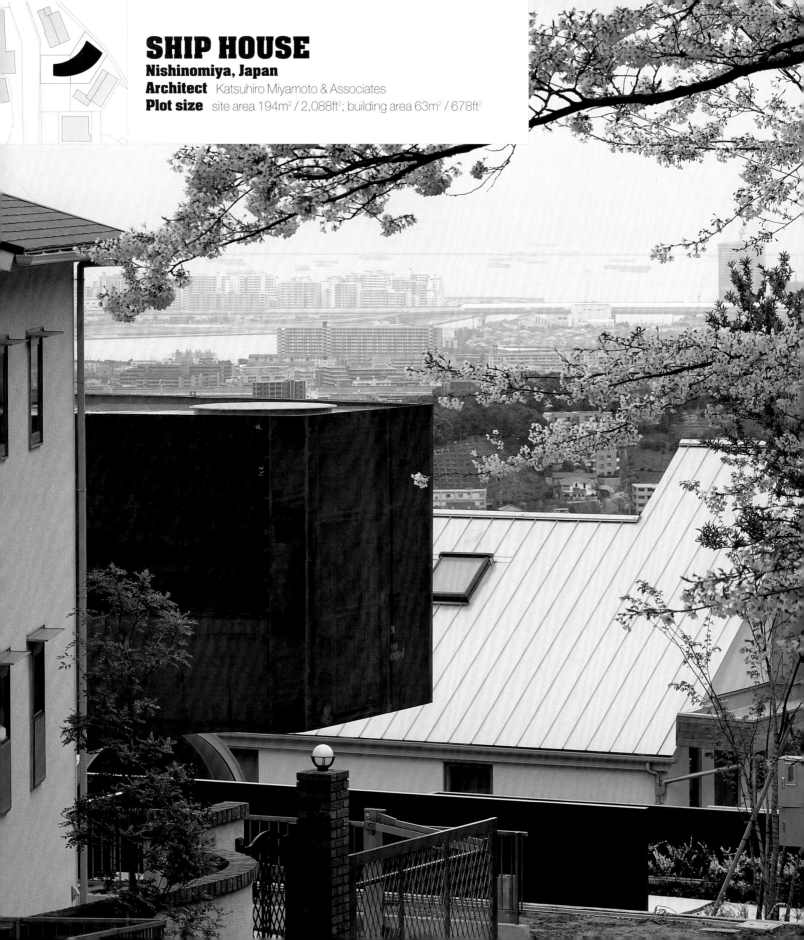

SHIP HOUSE
Nishinomiya, Japan
Architect Katsuhiro Miyamoto & Associates
Plot size site area 194m² / 2,088ft²; building area 63m² / 678ft²

1 A Cor-ten steel box sits between conventional homes on a quiet sloping street in Hyogo.

2 Section shows the two-tiered site with a level difference of 3 metres (10 feet).

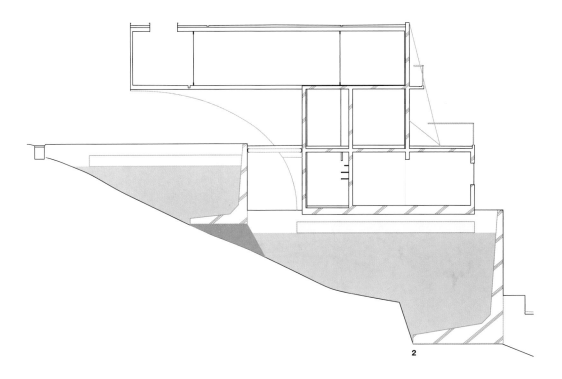

2

A ferry boat was the inspiration for this remarkable house which emerges out of a steep slope in the quiet residential neighbourhood of Nishinomiya in Japan's Hyogo prefecture.

The awkward L-shaped plot, owned by husband and wife Yoshio and Kiyoko Koyanagi, slopes three metres (ten feet) from the street in two tiers and is surrounded by houses on either side. A retaining wall has been constructed to shore up the embankment. When architect Katsuhiro Miyamoto was asked by the couple to build a home that could overcome this difficult terrain his solution was to build a three-tier structure in which the top tier would 'float' over the retaining wall.

The basement and ground floor are supported on a reinforced-concrete foundation that was laid on the lower and more stable portion of the site. Private spaces – a bedroom, study and bathroom – are located in the basement where the atmosphere is calm and at a distance from the street.

The vessel-like top tier projects over the front garden and houses the living room and kitchen with views over the neighbourhood from a rectangular window. Its curved form responds to the site's concave shape and effectively supports the large steel volume. Miyamoto used untreated panels of Cor-ten steel for the structure so over time it will take on a stable rust finish.

At street level there is an entrance to the house off a gravel carport, which connects a series of internal and external spaces leading to a terrace at the back. The result, according to Miyamoto, is 'reminiscent of a ferry boat, in terms of both structure and layout, in which passenger decks and floating sections are separated up and down with the vehicle decks in between'.

In contrast to the Cor-ten steel, the internal walls and ceilings are all painted white with small vertical openings and two skylights creating a light, calm and serene interior.

3 The steel 'vessel' cantilevers over the retaining wall of this steep site. Supporting the building are raft foundations located 3 metres (10 feet) below the entrance level. The bent volume is constructed and enclosed with panels of 12mm Cor-ten steel.

4 From left: Basement, ground- and first-floor plans. (1) bedroom, (2) study, (3) bathroom, (4) closet, (5) entrance, (6) children's room, (7) roof deck, (8) tatami room, (9) kitchen, (10) living/ dining, (11) inner balcony.

5 The curved building form responds to the L-shaped site. An entrance off the gravel carport takes you through to an entry hall and stairs to the first floor kitchen and living room.

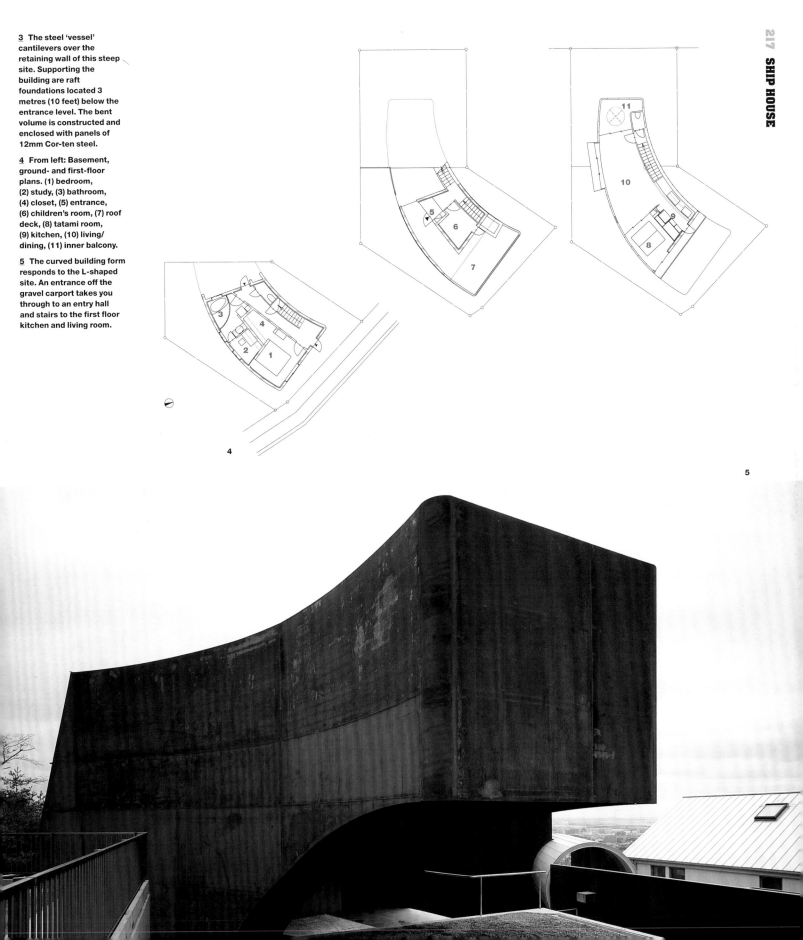

4

5

6 The fluid interior spaces are painted white in direct contrast to the rusted steel exterior. A rectangular window provides views across the neighbourhood.

7 Skylights and porthole windows bring in natural light and evoke the feeling of being inside a passenger ferry boat.

7

FAMILY HOUSE IN HINWIL
Hinwil, Switzerland
Architect Beat Rothen Architektur
Building footprint 113m² / 1,216ft²

1 Clockwise from top left: South, west, north and east elevations.

2 The house was designed as a decorative object in the landscape; the client, an artist, specified its crimson skin.

This three-storey family house occupies part of a garden subdivided from a large property in Hinwil, a small Alpine town about 30 kilometres (18½ miles) outside of Zurich in northeast Switzerland.

Its asymmetrical form is a response to the embankment that runs through the site (from northwest to southeast), the local land use ratio and the orientation of the building to minimize its impact on neighbouring properties.

There was no requirement for the house to mimic any of its immediate neighbours, a heterogeneous collection of buildings. Instead it was designed as a decorative object in the landscape. The client, an artist, specified its bright crimson skin.

The house has a thick concrete skeleton, which means that it has few loadbearing walls and retains heat effectively in the winter. The skeleton is wrapped in heat-insulated lightweight components and finished in plastic foil.

Glazing has been used extensively on the two upper

3 The building's complex form is a response to the embankment that runs through the site, the position of neighbouring properties and the ambition to create a strong statement in a heterogeneous suburban neighbourhood.

4 East–west section.

5 From left: Plans of the lower ground-floor (entrance), ground-floor (sleeping) and first-floor (living) levels.

levels: large picture windows frame views of the immediate landscape and the Alps on the top storey, and natural light floods into openings in each of the four rooms on the upper ground level. In areas of the house overlooked by neighbours, windows take the form of narrow slits in the wall.

The kitchen and communal living spaces are located on the top storey, to capitalize on the beautiful views and capture natural light. The unusual shape of the ceiling and the slanted walls creates the sense of being in an oversized tent.

In the centre of the top storey a staircase of exposed concrete offers access to the upper ground level, which is divided in two halves: one comprising two double bedrooms connected by a dressing room and bathroom; the other incorporating the children's room and a study. Sliding partition walls make it quick and easy to reconfigure the space as a single volume.

The lower ground level comprises a garage, large foyer, workshop and utility room.

4

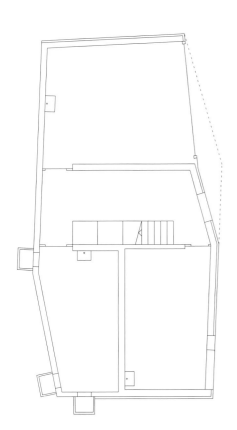
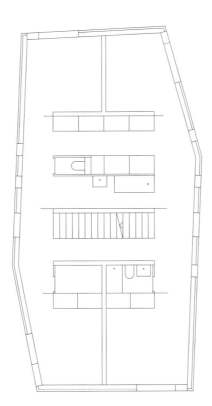
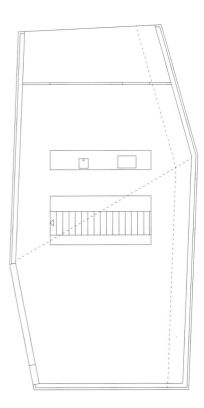

5

6

7

6 The exposed concrete staircase in the centre of the top-floor living area offers access to the bedroom and study on the level below.

7 Three bedrooms and a study are located on the upper ground level, which becomes a single space when the sliding doors are pulled open.

8 Large picture windows in the top-floor living area frame views of the Alps and the immediate landscape.

9 Slanted walls and the unusually shaped ceiling create a tent-like atmosphere on the top floor.

8

9

LIVING ROOM
Gelnhausen, Germany
Architect seifert.stoeckmann
Plot size 60m² / 646ft²

1 Building regulations required that the new house replicate the scale and form of the medieval timber-framed structure that previously occupied the site.

2 Front elevation: 52 windows punctuate the monolithic aluminium shell.

3 A large limestone boulder was imported from a quarry 200 kilometres (124 miles) away to create the ground floor.

2

3

The historic core of Gelnhausen, a trading town founded in 1180, is a conservation area. Much of the existing urban fabric dates from the late seventeenth century, a period during which the town underwent extensive reconstruction following the carnage wrought by the Thirty Years War (1618–48).

For obvious reasons, opportunities to build new houses in Gelnhausen are rare. So when the old Zitrone'hausche (Lemon House), a timber-framed structure at number 15 Kuhgasse, fell into terminal disrepair, it was too good an opportunity for architects Gabriela Seifert and Goetz Stoeckmann to pass up, especially as both of them knew the town from their school days.

Conservation regulations required that any new building on the asymmetrical site – which slopes north to south and is bordered on two sides by existing buildings – replicate the form and scale of the Zitrone'hausche. The building's envelope achieves this. But in most other respects the new house is a

world away from its predecessor. The house negates the usual distinction between inside and outside, public and private. The roof and the walls, inside and out, are all covered with the same unifying material. A rigorous grid of windows punctures the building shell.

Seifert and Stoeckmann designed the ground floor around an enormous limestone boulder, imported from a quarry near the Luxembourg border, 200 kilometres (124 miles) away. Aside from the boulder, all that occupies the ground floor are smaller boulders and a floor of loose gravel chips rather like a dried-up river bed. It offers some indication of the architects' conceptual approach to the house. Seifert explains: 'It is based on a threefold sectional concept. The ground floor is earthbound by the rock; a miniature "horizon" is created by the rock's four edges. The top deck on the box is open to the skies. The private spaces and their features inside the box refer to the journey of life …'

The interior is one large volume extending the full height of the building. Two factors facilitate this epic

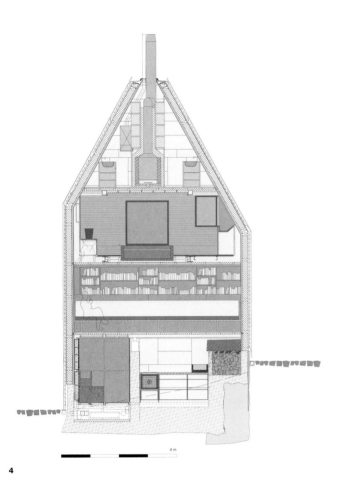

void: the integration of all the services, including the pantry, kitchen and a toilet, into the rear wall; and the suspension of the box from the gable walls. The entire space is flooded with natural light through 52 windows.

A minimally furnished living space, with two white sofas at the rear and a cowhide mat at the front, occupies the top floor – views of the boulder in the ground floor are visible through gaps on either side.

The level inside the box contains a generous boat-shaped bathtub and bedroom, and also contains arguably the defining feature of this extremely unusual building. The drawer-like box is supported on metal rails, which allow it to slide out of the front of the building. As well as being a metaphor for the journey of life, it is an ingenious means of creating an external balcony with views over the town; a concealed pressure pad in the floor activates the electric mechanism.

4

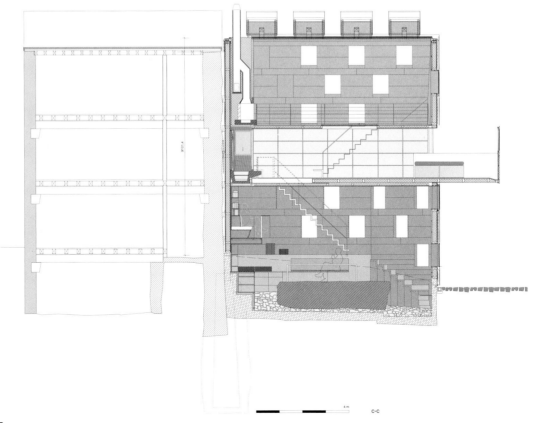

5

4 North–south section.

5 East–west section. Note the boulder in the basement, and the 'drawer' in the centre of the building.

6 An external balcony with views over historic Gelnhausen can be created at the touch of a button; the drawer-like box supported on metal rails protrudes from the front of the building.

7 All the upper levels are suspended from the gable walls; the kitchen below can be seen through the openings on either side of the minimally furnished gable floor.

8 Plan of the ground floor showing the shape of the boulder.

9 Ground-floor kitchen and dining area with raised boulder. All services, including the pantry, kitchen and toilet, are integrated into the rear wall.

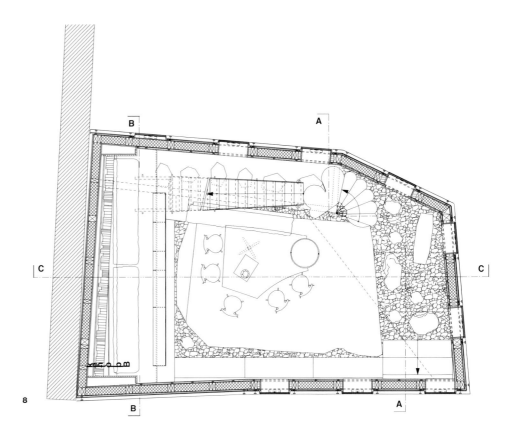

8

9

15½ CONSORT ROAD
Concept architect Paxton Locher
www.rparch.com
Project architect MOOArc
Fit-out architect FlowerMichelin

24 RUE DU BUISSON SAINT-LOUIS
Architect Christian Pottgiesser
www.pottgiesser.fr

302 STATION STREET
Architect Graeme Gunn Architects
www.graemegunn.com.au
Project Team Graeme Gunn, Bruce Rowe,
John McAuley
Engineer Dale Simpson, Perrett Simpson
Engineers
Builder Thylacine Constructions Pty Ltd.

AAG HOUSE
Architects Manuel Cerdá Pérez, Julio Vila Liante
www.mcparquitectura.com
Client Ana Alcacer Garcia
Technical architect Miguel Monteagudo
Cuevas

BRICK HOUSE
Architects FKL architects (Diarmuid Brophy,
Michelle Fagan, Paul Kelly, Gary Lysaght,
Sterrin O'Shea)
www.fklarchitects.com
Quantity surveyors Bruce Shaw Partnership
Engineers DBFL Consulting Engineers
Main contractor JPK Building Contractors

BROOKES STREET HOUSE
Architect James Russell Architect
www.jamesrussellarchitect.com.au
Builder James Russell
Engineer Bligh Tanner Consulting Engineers

DUONG HOUSE
Architect Philippe Villien
www.villien.com
Exploratory assistant A.J. Martinon
Client Duc Duong
Engineer David Chambolle
Economist M. Poix
**Steel construction, external woodwork,
siding** PMB, M. Oger
Masonry Frank Messana
Electricity Monnier
Imperviousness Scopase

DRYER HOUSE
**Architect, construction management and
interior designer** BKK-3
www.bkk-3.com
Project management Franz Sumnitsch
Assistants Dominik Hennecke, Tina Krischmann,
Hendrik Steinigeweg, Christine Huber,
Johnny Winter
Owner Family Lamm-Dreier

EUCLID AVENUE HOUSE
Architect Levitt Goodman Architects (Janna Levitt,
Dean Goodman, Danny Bartman)
www.levittgoodmanarchitects.com
Structural engineer Kasey Bartusevicius, G.D.
Jewell Engineering Inc.
Landscaping/green Roof Terry McGlade,
Perennial Gardens Corp.
Construction manager Boszko and Verity Inc.

FAIRVIEW AVENUE RESIDENCE
Architect David Neiman Architects
www.neimanarchitects.com
Owner Annie Rosen
Builder Joe McKinstry Construction Company
Engineer Harriott Smith Valentine Engineers, Inc.

FAMILY HOUSE NEAR LIÈGE
Architect Atelier d'Architecture Marc Grondal
Principal-in-charge Eric Grondal
Project team Eric Grondal
Client Thierri Grondal
Structural engineer Bureau d'Etudes Lemaire
sprl
General contractor Antoine Pirenne sprl

FAMILY HOUSE IN HINWIL
Architect Beat Rothen Architektur GmbH
www.beatrothen.ch
Strucural engineer Dubach & Wittwer AG
Heating and sanitation engineer Russo
Haustechnik AG
Lighting engineer Vogt & Partner

FAMILY HOUSE IN VICHY
Architect Rémi Laporte (with logistical help from
Philip Martin's office)
Structure Edouard Tereszkiewicz (12C-Pingat)
Thermal Guicheret office

FENNELL RESIDENCE
Architect Robert Harvey Oshatz
www.oshatz.com

FOCUS HOUSE
Architect bere:architects
www.bere.co.uk
Client Edward Gibbs
Contractors Vision Build Ltd
Structural engineer Techniker
Specialist subcontractor (solid timber
structure) KLH UK
Specialist subcontractor (zinc) PMF Roofcraft
Quantity surveyor Andrew Turner Company
Landscape architects Buckley Design
Associates

FORT GREENE HOUSE
Architect Christoff:Finio
www.christofffinio.com
Principals-in-charge Taryn Christoff,
Martin Finio
Project manager Jeff Hong
Structural engineer Severud Associates

GOLDEN NUGGET
Architect INNOCAD Planung und
Projektmanagement GmbH (Martin Lesjak,
Andreas Reiter, Peter Schwaiger,
Bernd Steinhuber)
www.innocad.at
Project manager Martin Krammer
Assistance Roland List, Alexander Gruber,
Clemens Luser
Client 99 PLUS Projektentwicklung und Bauträger
GmbH
Structural consultant DI Gerhard Baumkirchner
Façade Steinbauer Ges.mbH
Roof Steinbauer Ges.mbH
Masonry Herzog Baugesellschaft mbH & Co. KG
Doors KTB Holzverarbeitungsbetriebe Ges.mbH
TECU® Gold cladding KM Europa Metal AG
Services Kindermann Bad-Heiztechnik Ges.mbH
Electrical services Elektro Bauer
Plumbing Kindermann Bad-Heiztechnik Ges.mbH
Heating, ventilation, air-conditioning
Kindermann Bad-Heiztechnik Ges.mbH
Lighting planning, fittings INNOCAD Planung
und Projektmanagement
Windows VELUX Österreich GmbH
Flooring Bscheider GmbH
Furnishings INNOCAD Planung und
Projektmanagement, M. Eberhart, Inside
Graphic design Superplus Entertainment
Print on fabric Bergmann GmbH
Curtains Rautnigg & Co.

HILL HOUSE
Architect Johnston Marklee & Associates;
Mark Lee (principal-in-charge), Sharon Johnston
AIA, Jeff Adams & Mark Rea Baker (project
architects); Diego Arraigada, Brennan Buck,
Michelle Cintron, Daveed Kapoor, Anne
Rosenberg, Anton Schneider (project team)
www.johnstonmarklee.com
Developer Lucas Ma, President, Markee LLC
Owner Chan Luu
Contractor Hinerfeld-Ward, Inc.
Structural engineer William Koh & Associates
Landscape Lush Life LA
Lighting consultant Dan Weinreber

HOUSE IN MONTMARTRE
Architect Tomoko Anyoji + Yannick Beltrando
architects, Laurent Castanet architect
Engineer GDMH, (foundation) SAFA,
(RC structure) ARDEN, (metallic structure)

HP HOUSE
Architects Akira Yoneda/architecton and
Masahiro Ikeda/Masahiro Ikeda Co., Ltd
www.architecton.co.jp
www.miascoltd.net

LIVING ROOM
Architecture/landscape Gabriela Seifert and
Goetz Stoeckmann, seifert.stoeckmann with
Martin Boehler, Jan Peter Dahl, Serge Dahouk,
Marco Hofmann, Roland Schnizer
www.formalhaut.de
Structural engineering Eugen Schuler
Structural engineering Heinz Pfefferkorn
Environmental engineering Heiner Lupprian
with Heim, Bietzke, Höfer
Painting Ludger Gerdes
Photography Ottmar Hörl
Relief/sculpture Georg Hüter
Lyrics Thomas Kling
Sculpture Wolfgang Luy
Installation Scott Murff
Pottery Christine Neidlinger
Installation Catherine Spellman
Light Charly Steiger
Noise Achim Wollscheid
Earthworks Nees
Concrete works Kaufmann
Timber frame Helmut Feuerstein
Steel works/drawer Josef Martin
Electrical services Dotzauer
Heating/water/air supply Wernig
Cabinetmaker Balzer
Cabinet maker Leder
Rock(s) Schmitz
Sponsorship City of Gelnhausen, BEGA,
Louis Poulsen

LIVE/WORK HOUSE
Architect de Leeuw + van Zanten together with
DAAD Architecten
www.deleeuwvanzanten.nl
www.daad.nl
Projectarchitect Eric de Leeuw
Client Hoogland & Versteegh

LOVE HOUSE
Architect Takeshi Hosaka Architects
www.hosakatakeshi.com

LOWERLINE HOUSE

Architect Byron Mouton, bild Design
www.bildit.com
Contractor Anthony Christiana
Construction crew A.J. Christiana Construction
Millwork Dean Kageler
Metal specialties Sam Richards

LUCKY DROPS

Architect Yasuhiro Yamashita (Atelier Tekuto) with Masahiro Ikeda (Masahiro Ikeda Co., Ltd)
www.tekuto.com
Construction Hideo Kikushima (Kikushima Co., Ltd), with the cooperation of Shigeki Matsuoka (Home Builder)

MICHAELIS HOUSE

Architect Alex Michaelis, Michaelis Boyd Associates
www.michaelisboyd.com
Project team Alex Michaelis, Tim Boyd, Rodrigo Moreno Masey
Structural engineer P&N
Mechanical engineer Arup

NATURAL WEDGE

Architects Masaki Endoh + Masahiro Ikeda / Endoh Design House EDH + mias
www.edh-web.com
Principal-in-charge Rio Tomita, Kenji Nawa, Hirofumi Ohno
General contractor RIDEA CONSTRUCTION Co., Ltd

OLD HOUSE

Architects Jackson Clements Burrows Pty Ltd Architects
www.jcba.com.au
Project team Jon Clements, Tim Jackson, Graham Burrows, Kim Stapleton, Josh Flavell, Tim Humphries
Engineer Meyer Consulting
Builder BD Projects
Landscape architect Emma Ferguson (Mantello)
Building surveyor Australian Building Permits
Façade image High Performance Films
Façade glazing Ascott Glass
Client David Clements
Heating/cooling systems Griepink & Ward
Benchtops Rutso Concrete
Joinery Cattanach Kitchens
Kitchen appliances Smeg

ONE WINDOW HOUSE

Architect Touraine Richmond Architects
www.touraine-richmond.com
Design team Terri Moore, Deborah Richmond, Olivier Touraine, Taiyo Watanabe
Structural engineering Anders Carlson, Gilsanz Murray Steficek
Builder Bruce Brown, Brown Osvaldsson Builders
Landscape design Touraine Richmond Architects
Curtains/textiles Cathy Pack

PANEL HOUSE

Project designer/project architect David Hertz, FAIA, LEED A.P./ John Meachem
Project managers Keith Ireland, Lucas Goettsche, Jared Wright
General contractor Ron Senso Construction
Structural engineer C.W. Howe Partners Inc.
Mechanical Monterey Energy Group (MEG)

ROOFTECTURE S

Architect Shuhei Endo Architect Institute
www.paramodern.com
Consultants Masashi Ooji, Design-Structure Laboratory

SHIP HOUSE

Architect Katsuhiro Miyamoto & Associates
www.kmaa.jp
Principal-in-charge Katsuhiro Miyamoto
Project team Kazuhiro Takeuchi
Collaborator Masahiro Miyake / y+M design office
Structural engineering Masaichi Taguchi / TAPS
General contractor Yamamoto Komuten
Steel construction Nakamitsu Kenko, Mukai Tekkojo

SÁNCHEZ MEDINA HOUSE

Architect Manuel de las Casas
Collaborators Iciar de las Casas (architect), Sergio de las Casas (structures)
Assistants P. Enfedaque, L. McNicholl, R. Heras, P. García, J. McNicholl
Collaborator Eusebio Sánchez (quantity surveyor)
Client Sres Sánchez Medina
Construction company Alfonso Peña, S.L.

SKY TRACE

Architect Kiyoshi Sey Takeyama + AMORPHE
www.amorphe.jp
Principal in charge Ikuma Yoshizawa
Structural engineer K3 Structure Design Office, Hirofumi Kaneko
Mechanical engineer Soh Mechanical Engineers, Masami Tanno, Akhiro Nanjo
Contractor Sobi

STAIRCASE HOUSE
Architect exe.arquitectura
www.exearquitectura.com
Technical architect Jordi Roig
Installation engineer Imego 2000 s.l.
Structure Codi Arquitectura
Builder L'Ocefo s.l.
Smith Morace
Interior carpentry Disseny Oricar
Façade Vip Metall
Installations Imego 2000
Kitchen Artificio
Lighting Gaudir il luminacio
Furniture Ego sofas, Arkitektura, Dae, En Linea
   Barcelona
Ceramics Acocsa
Wood flooring Schotten & Hansen
Bathroom fittings Architect

SUNKEN HOUSE
Architect Adjaye Associates
www.adjaye.com
Structural engineer (superstructure) and
   contractor (superstructure)
   Eurban.Construction
Contractor (groundworks) Wallace
   Contractors
Client Ed Reeve

TOWN HOUSE
Architects KRISCHPARTNER
www.krischpartner.de
Partner-in-charge Rüdiger Krisch
Project manager Gerald Goldbach
Structural consultant U. Ströbel
Mechanical consultant T. Efferenn
Electrical consultant G. Hölldampf

URBAN INFILL 01
Architect Johnsen Schmaling Architects
www.johnsenschmaling.com
Client Blue Sky Developments
Structural engineer Patera, LLC

VERTICAL HOUSE
Architect Lorcan O'Herlihy Architects
www.loharchitects.com
Principal-in-charge Lorcan O'Herlihy
Project team David Thompson, Kevin Tsai
Client Lorcan O'Herlihy & Cornelia Hayes O'Herlihy